FIRST THINGS FIRST

GROWING IN PASTORAL MINISTRY

by
Ken Kamau

HIPPOBOOKS

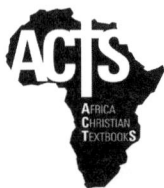

Copyright © 2016 by Ken Kamau

Published 2016 by HippoBooks, an imprint of WordAlive, ACTS, Langham Creative Projects and Zondervan.

Africa Christian Textbooks (ACTS), TCNN, PMB 2020, Bukuru 930008, Plateau State, Nigeria. **www.africachristiantextbooks.com**

Langham Creative Projects, PO Box 296, Carlisle, Cumbria, CA3 9WZ, UK. **www.langhamcreative.org**

WordAlive Publishers, PO Box 4547, GP0-00100 Nairobi, Kenya **www.wordalivepublishers.com**

Zondervan, 3900 Sparks Dr. SE., Grand Rapids, Michigan 49546. **www.zondervan.com**

Library of Congress Cataloging-in-Publication Data

Names: Kamau, Ken, author.
Title: First things first : growing in pastoral ministry : / by Ken Kamau.
Description: Grand Rapids : Zondervan, 2016.
Identifiers: LCCN 2016013122 | ISBN 9789966003829 (softcover)
Subjects: LCSH: Pastoral theology.
Classification: LCC BV4011.3 .K36 2016 | DDC 253—dc23 LC record available at
    http://lccn.loc.gov/2016013122

Cover design: **projectluz.com**

Book design: To a Tee Ltd, **www.2at.com**

16 17 18 19 20 21 22 23 24 25 26 /DHV/ 15 14 13 12 11 10 9 8 7 6 5 4 3 2 1

FIRST THINGS FIRST

I dedicate this book to three godly women in my life:
My grandmother, who led me to the Lord
My mother, a pillar of faith
My wife, a woman of wisdom and unwavering commitment

CONTENTS

ACKNOWLEDGMENTS

This book is a reflection of the journey I have walked, a journey that only found meaning and purpose at the foot of the cross. My first thanks is to Jesus Christ who loved me when I was still afar off, called me, and wrote my name in his Book of Life. His unconditional love has kept me going even when the road is tough.

Thanks to my wife, best friend and partner in ministry, Wacuka. She has made our journey in ministry an adventure. Her prayer, passion and dedication to seeing this book finished inspired me to keep writing even during the not-so-good times.

To my two wonderful children, Nathan and Nyambura – God has used you to teach me more about leadership than any other book.

To the elders of Kileleshwa Covenant Community Church for entrusting me with leadership where few would have done so. Thank you for giving me the space and freedom to dream big and lead with confidence, knowing you have my back.

To the Tandaza staff team – thank you for choosing to join me in this ministry adventure. Your dedication and commitment to Christ have taught me great leadership lessons.

To the Kileleshwa Church intercessory team led by Kendi Ogamba – thank you for constantly being on your knees during the writing of this book.

To the congregations of Kileleshwa Covenant, Tandaza Celebration Centre, and Shepherds Green – thank you for allowing me to walk with you in this faith adventure.

To the many more churches we will see planted to the glory of God.

To Rev. Peter and Beth Njogah and the Deliverance Church, Ongata Rongai, where my journey started.

To Glenmore Park Anglican Church in Australia and the wonderful congregation for being the hands and feet of Christ.

To the team at HippoBooks, who made this possible by extending trust and creating a platform for authors. And to Isobel Stevenson and her editorial team extraordinaire.

And finally to Pastor Oscar Muriu and Pastor Muriithi Wanjau, two men who have been instrumental in shaping me and daring me to trust the Lord for more.

1

INTRODUCTION

Pastors or leaders never start their ministry with the aim of failing or disappointing those who have given them the role and responsibility of leadership.

I remember, during my time at Bible college, many of the conversations were about what we called the ABC's of ministry – Attendance, Building and Cash. Pastors loved talking about the congregation sizes of various churches, the property they owned, and the offerings in those big churches.

Most of us, if not all of us, dreamt and planned to be leaders of big churches or ministries.

Visionary leaders dream big. They spend time churning ideas of how things can be; they do not see the obstacles or the challenges. In fact, obstacles and challenges fuel their desire to do grand things.

We see these leaders take youth ministries by storm or plant churches that grow and thrive where others have failed. We are mesmerized at how easily and quickly they build a core and how easily they rally people around them. We want to be part of their team, their church, their inner circle; we want to understand how they think and work. We also come across great strategic thinkers or worship pastors, preachers and children's pastors all of whom we love and are captivated by.

Having interacted with a number of great pastors, I know that Africa is blessed with visionary leaders in the church arena. I think of men like Pastor Oscar Muriu of Nairobi Chapel, Bishop Arthur Gitonga of Redeemed Church, Archbishop Wabukala of the Anglican Church, Archbishop Ben Kwashi from Nigeria and Rev. Phineas Dube of Zimbabwe, to mention only a few.

However, in this beautifully created being, driven by a gospel conviction, consumed by love for the lost, there lies a dark side, that is selfish, broken, and desperately wicked – a part ruled by sin!

Sin works at robbing us of what God has promised; it works at redirecting us to self-destruction, annihilation and a complete falling short of God's expectations.

It still surprises me how I and many others are still shocked by the fall of great men and women who are giants in ministry. We see young and old leaders come in and do great exploits for God. But after a while we hear that they have left the church they were leading broken, split and full of in-fighting. Or we are treated to unending dramas involving financial or moral scandals, and we ask ourselves what happened to the passionate leader we all admired.

Some of those who fall may be people we thought of as insignificant members of the community. But others are those we considered worthy of the title "Man of God" or "Woman of God", people with a coveted place in society, whom we looked up to with admiration, respect and awe, and whom we desperately wanted to emulate. We may even have modelled our ministries and careers on theirs. Then one day we are rocked by the news that they have fallen or been captured by that dreaded monster Sin. How did it happen? Why? It cannot be; it's impossible! How could such a great and passionate leader fall?

We go into a state of shock, followed by denial and then spiritual depression. Those on the edge looking for a chance to discredit the faith leap with joy at such opportunities. Some use these incidents as excuses for why they will never believe in or follow such a damaged faith.

In order to save face, we look for every possible reason to excuse the falling of the man or woman of God. We say it's the stress of ministry (blaming God and the church); others may say it's the strain of being in the limelight (blaming society).

But why, even after so many examples and stories, do people still get caught quite literally with their pants down? How come the many passionate leaders at the back of the line, just graduating from Bible school, planting churches, or taking up lead positions in churches don't learn from these life lessons? Can this cycle be broken?

In this book, I share lessons I have learnt over the last ten or so years as I have moved from being a youth volunteer in a small church in a small town to being asked to lead a church that was divided, broken and hurting when I was twenty-eight years old. I have faced many challenges, but I have also seen the Lord graciously work in this church, so that today it is growing and healthy and has even planted other churches.

As I started out to lead this church, I read many books on leadership in a desperate attempt to feel more equipped for this challenging new role. Yet many of the books I read were by authors who were either far ahead in the ministry journey or far removed from my African context. So most of the wonderful truths in these books were either abstract or impossible to grasp because of where I was in life and the issues that mattered most to me at that time.

I was asking questions and reading books that gave me great answers to questions that would matter at a different season. I was asking questions about how to build a team with a zero budget, how to lead a congregation that was broken, how to get buy-in and permission to lead a congregation whose average age was ten to fifteen years older than I was. I felt like Ezekiel in the valley of dry bones reflecting on God's question, "Can these bones live?" (Ezek 37:3). My life was the valley and my leadership skills were the dry bones.

When I look back over the brief period I have been allowed to lead, I can honestly say it's only now, ten years later, that some truths I read about are starting to make sense.

I have been very blessed in my leadership journey. In the short span of these ten years I have enjoyed the great satisfaction of growing in leadership on the fast track because of a few great men and women that the Lord brought into my life all in different seasons and for reasons. Some of these relationships were hard and uncomfortable and I would rather forget them, but the lessons were invaluable. Some still continue to date and others changed my life over a cup of coffee.

These individuals made the journey not easier but clearer. Having spent time with other young and emerging African leaders, I know for a fact that having people walk with you is not the norm, so I count myself blessed!

As I look back on those years, I remember a conversation the prophet Jeremiah had with God. Jeremiah was complaining about the prosperity of the wicked and wondering whether God has forgotten about his prophet and his people. God's answer was simple but mind-blowing:

> If you have raced with men on foot, and they have worn you out, how will you compete with horses? If you stumble in safe country, how will you manage in the thickets by the Jordan? (Jer 12:5)

Basically if you are struggling with the small-time things and they are wearing you out, how will you do in the big leagues? If you want to be a blessing to the kingdom, you have to get the basics right. Before you step into the spotlight of ministry life, you need to work in the backstage of life.

My prayer is that as you step into your definition of successful ministry, you will be ready and will honour God by not bringing shame to the name of Christ.

I pray this book is a blessing to you and your ministry.

2

EVERYONE HAS A VILLAGE

Everyone has a place of beginning, what I call our "village". To help you understand what I mean, let me tell you about a counselling case that baffled me for a while.

A young couple (let me call them Jane and John) had come to me for advice on some marital challenges they were going through. As I listened and engaged with them, I realized that I needed more time with the husband so I could get his perspective on what was going on.

The bottom line was that a few years into the marriage they had both been financially blessed. They decided it was time to start buying the house they had talked about during courtship.

When they were dating, Jane had a better paying job and John was struggling in-between jobs. So she had helped with most of the wedding expenses and their expenses in the first year of their marriage.

John's career had eventually got on track and he was now earning significantly more than Jane. But while the income scales had changed, the responsibility scales had not. John still wanted to do what he had been doing with his earlier inconsistent salary, leaving Jane to cover the major expenses.

But this was not what brought them for counselling. The real issue was what John spent his money on. His baffled wife could not comprehend the amounts he spent and the things he spent them on.

Hence my decision to spend time with him and find out more.

As we had coffee, John told me about his childhood. He grew up in an extremely poor family with a single mother. Her priority was to get him and his siblings through high school. As for university, they would each have to work their way through that one.

So throughout his primary and high school years, John never had a new shirt, new shoes or even new underwear. His school uniform was always either a gift from a graduating student or bought second-hand. His mother would ensure that all the torn parts were well patched.

Because of having to work and go to university at the same time, he graduated two years after most of his classmates. But in his final year he met and fell in love with Jane, who reminded him of his mum, strong-willed, never shaken and able to make anything out of nothing.

Fast forward to the present, and now for the first time in his life John had a job that paid him better than all his friends. For the first time in his life he could walk into a shop and buy a new shirt, new shoes, a watch and a suit.

What started off as a subtle realization that he could actually do this grew into an unquenchable obsession with buying new things. He could not explain why he had twenty-nine suits in his wardrobe, or why he had over thirty pairs of shoes or ten different watches, some of which he had never removed from the box they came in.

There is nothing wrong with having new suits, watches or shoes; the problem in this case was the motive for buying them. The ability to buy new things gave him a sense of power and standing among his friends and workmates. So when Jane demanded that he take more financial responsibility, she was asking him to do something that would leave him with less disposable income to buy new things. He saw this as going back to a place of powerlessness and dependence.

Why did I introduce this story with a reference to the "village"?

Everyone has a place of beginning, what I call a "village". It is the place where we begin; the place where we take our baby steps in ministry and leadership. In the case of King David, his starting point in leadership was Bethlehem. It was his first classroom; it was in this place that he was launched from the obscurity that was shepherding into the limelight that was kingship.[1] It was a place of discovery and new beginnings.

And just like King David we all have a village. If you look back at your life, you will remember some place of which you can say, "That's where I started out", whether in business, in your corporate career or in ministry.

---

[1] Ronald. E. Cottle, *Anointed to Reign: David's Pathway to Rulership* (Shippensburg, Penn: Destiny Image Publishers, 1996), 5.

My "village" was a local church in the small town of Ongata Rongai. It was there I discovered my leadership gifts, learnt some of ministry's greatest lessons, was given my first opportunity to preach in the adult service, and was entrusted with the youth ministry. It was there that I failed many, many times, and also learnt to get up and push on, all in the safety of a loving and understanding community that knew me inside out. They knew my intentions were true even when I goofed up big time.

Your "village" may be the place where you were a leader in high school, or a volunteer in the local village church, or maybe part of a youth mission team in university. Wherever it was that you had that conviction and desire to serve the Lord, that is the place I call your village.

Your village may look very insignificant, but the lessons you learnt there are vital to who you have become.

If you look at significant people in the Bible, you will realize that they all had a "Bethlehem" or starting point. For Moses it was a floating basket picked up by Pharaoh's daughter; for Joseph it was a dream and then a well; for Samuel it was as a boy in the temple; for Peter the fisherman it was the Sea of Galilee; for Christ it was the manger.

I want you to look back at where you started. Can you clearly answer the question: What is or was my village?

I believe many of the challenges we are dealing with in the church in Africa lie in the foundations from which pastors launched into leadership and ministry. When you see cracks starting to appear in a house, the cracks are not the problem; they are just the result of a house having been poorly built. This is what Matthew 7:24–27 tells us:

> Everyone then who hears these words of mine and does them will be like a wise man who built his house on the rock. And the rain fell, and the floods came, and the winds blew and beat on that house, but it did not fall, because it had been founded on the rock. And everyone who hears these words of mine and does not do them will be like a foolish man who built his house on the sand. And the rain fell, and the floods came, and the winds blew and beat against that house, and it fell, and great was the fall of it.

When we have heavy rain overnight and we wake up to flooded houses and impassable roads, it is not the rain that is the problem. Someone somewhere either did not design the drainage system well or the drainage system is all clogged up.

So when we see, read or hear of "men and women of God" who have fallen let us look beyond the unfolding crises, look beyond the fruit, beyond the stem, beyond the branch, beyond the trunk and focus on the roots, for therein lies the problem.

One of the challenges I faced when I agreed to take up the lead role in this hurting church was remaining true to who I was and what I believed to be central to shepherding with integrity and intentionality. I was scared as I had never done this before, and in fear I quickly started reading all the leadership books I could get my hands on. I started looking for all the leadership books on leading a broken, hurting church. But over time I have learnt that it is always best to look back at your own leadership journey, the path the Lord has taken you through and the lessons you have learnt. That is where you will find answers to some of the most difficult leadership questions you will ask at every stage of your leadership journey. Every season, storm, celebration, battle, victory, defeat you have endured has a place in your current leadership journey.

When we choose not to remain true to who we are, we cave in to the pressure of the ABC's of ministry and start to shape our churches and ministries on the basis of our own insecurities and fears instead of on the basis of the vision and mandate given to us by God.

Back to the opening story: John certainly had a rough start to life, but the challenge the couple was facing was not financial but one of John's not being true to the lessons learnt in his place of beginning. He was ashamed of his past and had a sinking feeling that "as long as I can't afford it I am powerless".

Their story does have a happy ending though. After professional counselling John got over the shame of his past and turned it into lessons for others. As a bonus they are now able to afford their dream house.

Speaking to students who were graduating from Stanford University in California, Steve Jobs, the former CEO of Apple Computer and of

Pixar Animation Studios, told three stories about connecting the dots, love and loss, and death.[2]

In these stories he talks about learning life lessons though very tough times, like when he was fired from a company he founded. He also talks about major decisions he made and says that the path he walked only made sense much later in life.

But it is his first story on learning to connect the dots that captures what I have been talking about. He says that we must learn to look back on our life and start to see how the dots connect. Things that may seem irrelevant at one point will make total sense later on once we have connected the dots.

We must learn to connect the dots in our life journey because they may represent a silent whisper from the Lord giving us an answer to what we are asking now.

As I said at the start of this chapter, we all have a village, the place of our calling and beginning. What is your village?

In my village I learnt major lessons that have pushed me through many tough seasons, and I am still learning.

[2] Available online at news.stanford.edu/news/2005/june15/jobs-061505.html

3

SPIRITUAL AUTHORITY

The first lesson I learnt in my village was how to be under authority. The account of David and Samuel in 1 Samuel chapters 16 to 17 captures what I mean.

You will remember that after God rejects Saul, Samuel is in shock, as many of us are when a leader falls. If takes him quite some time to get over it. But then God tells him something very important: "I am sending you to Jesse of Bethlehem. I have chosen one of his sons to be king" (1 Sam 16:1).

So Samuel, still upset at Saul's rejection, goes to the house of Jesse to anoint the next king of Israel. And when he sees the first of Jesse's sons, Samuel is sure that he must be the one, for he is tall and looks kingly (1 Sam 16:6).

But God reveals a truth to Samuel. God looks beyond what is seen – the physical appearance – to the unseen – the heart.

David was the last-born of Jesse's sons. He was so insignificant that even after Samuel has asked Jesse to send for all his sons, they forgot David. He is later remembered as a by-the-way and they send for him. Imagine the shock on their faces when David was anointed king over Israel. It must have been a humbling and surreal occasion for them. What was going through Jesse's mind, or his sons' minds, as they found themselves standing around the one they considered the least important but who was being anointed king over Israel?

It is in this humble setting that David takes his first step into leadership.

It is interesting to note how God directs David towards his destiny. After David is anointed king, he does not run to set up a kingdom or challenge Saul. Instead, he goes back to tending his father's sheep (1 Sam 16:19).

What is even more interesting is that God in his divine strategy brings David into Saul's service because of his skill with the harp (1 Sam 16:16–18).

> "Let our lord command his servants here to search for someone who can play the lyre. He will play when the evil spirit from God comes on you, and you will feel better." So Saul said to his attendants, "Find someone who plays well and bring him to me." One of the servants answered, "I have seen a son of Jesse of Bethlehem who knows how to play the lyre. He is a brave man and a warrior. He speaks well and is a fine-looking man. And the LORD is with him." (1 Sam 16:16–18)

Now I'm sure that there were many people who played the harp in Israel and to get noticed by one of the king's attendants and called into the king's service you had to be pretty good.

It is in this setting that David learns a very important lesson on spiritual authority: His first step to his destiny as king of Israel was serving as a musician to the king.

Watchman Nee in his book *Spiritual Authority* states, "In God's work He sets some to be in authority with others to be under authority."[1] Leadership is about balancing these two tensions and knowing where you stand at different times. The moment you get these two mixed up is the moment you start to walk towards a cliff.

David must have understood this, which is why he obediently came under the authority of Saul even though he knew that God had anointed *him* king.

Many of us once we discover, or are told by others, that we have been called and anointed immediately demand or start relentlessly working to be appointed as king. We want everyone to know and recognize that we are called, anointed and highly favoured of God. We do not see the need to be under any authority. Why should we care? We are already called and anointed.

---

[1] Watchman Nee, *Spiritual Authority* (North Chesterfield, Vt.: Christian Fellowship Publishers, 1972), 30.

What makes submission even harder to endure is the fact that many times it is true that we could actually do a better job than the person who has authority over us.

Saul was not a loveable man at this point. It would have been easy enough to get reasons to plan a coup and set Israel free from this dejected king: he was leading them astray, he was constantly under demonic attack, the spirit of the Lord had left him (1 Sam 16:14).

But the truth is this: you will struggle with authority under you until you learn to have authority over you. Many great pastors fall simply because they refused to learn to be under authority.

God does not have secret lone rangers who show up and save an entire village. Nor does he have supermen or heroes who are faster than a speeding bullet and can take on an entire army by themselves and save the world. No! He has established order and community in the body of Christ, so that we live in submission first to Christ as the Head and then to those God has placed over us, and with one another. We all have to start somewhere, and it is never right at the top.

Every position of authority in the kingdom begins as a humble seat of servanthood.[2] The greater the authority, the greater the servant.

In John 13:1–17 Jesus makes this message very clear during the Last Supper. Though his disciples had walked with him for three years, they still struggled with the issue of servanthood and submitting to one another. This happened a few times and took various forms. For example, in Luke 22:24 we are told, "A dispute also arose among them as to which of them was considered to be greatest" (see also Mark 9:33–34; 10:35–45; Luke 9:46–48; Matthew 20:20–28). The apostles argued among themselves about which of them was greatest and would have the highest position in the kingdom. They had a serious problem with pride and self-exaltation.

Christ repeatedly taught them about true humility and submission. Mark's Gospel records his telling them "If anyone wants to the first, he must be the very last and servant of all" (Mark 9:35). The argument recorded in Luke 22:24 took place during the Last Supper. At a time when Jesus was troubled in spirit and preparing them for what was about to come, they were still having this argument about status! They

---

[2] Cottle, *Anointed to Reign*, 7.

still didn't get it. So Jesus demonstrated what he had been trying to teach them.

When they are all seated and ready to eat after a long and dusty journey, Jesus got up, removed his outer garments, put water in a basin and bowed down to wash their feet! (John 13:4–5). To understand how significant this was, foot-washing was a task reserved only for slaves.

This must have stung the entire group deeply. Can you imagine the shock, disbelief and silence as they watched their Lord and Master taking up the humble role of a slave to wash their dirty feet?

They are the ones who should have been washing his feet.

Peter refused to let him do this, but this refusal was not driven by humility but rather by guilt and, to some extent, pride. He as the leader of the team should have done this for his master, not the other way around.

Then Jesus asked the question, "Do you understand what I have done for you?" If he as Lord and Master did this for the disciples, who are we to say we cannot be in submission to those we are under?

You can never be in ministry what you do not become in your local church. In other words, the way you are in the local church (your village) maps out how you will become in the ministry (as a leader).

If in your local church you are always antagonistic, rebellious, lazy, inconsistent in your commitments, suspicious of the leadership above you, and so on, chances are that's the type of leader you will be.

You want to become a great pastor, learn to be a great follower, a great congregant and a faithful servant!

In our context, those in authority over us may include elders, supervisors, parents, and CEO's. Whatever authority God has put above you, you need to submit to it. It may not be the best authority to be under, but if you can learn to be faithful even under difficult leadership you will have learnt an invaluable leadership lesson.

I served in a certain church while I was in Bible school doing my BA in Bible and Theology. I was part of a team that was putting together an outreach and church-planting strategy for a new church plant. I had done this before with this same team. However, having gone to Bible school and started to read more widely, I now realized that there were better ways of doing church planting than we had done the previous two times. But the pastor I was under was more old-school and was not very keen to try new things or new strategies.

I started to feel frustrated with the same old conversations and strategies that had not worked in the past, trouble-shooting the same problems in the same way. I was now thinking of big words like "retention strategy", "leadership pipeline", and the like ... things I had read about in books and was now applying totally out of context. Only now do I realize how foolish I actually was!

My frustration started leaking through during meetings. I would ask questions not because I wanted to know the answer but because I wanted to expose the "lack of understanding" of the pastor I was under and to show that my idea was better. He had no Bible degree and was definitely not a strategic thinker like I was, or so I thought. Tension grew within the group and every meeting was very uncomfortable.

After one heated exchange, one of the elders asked that I remain behind. I rejoiced that at last someone had noticed how un-strategic we were.

But the conversation with the elder did not go the way I thought it would, and did not last as long as I thought it would. He simply said (paraphrased), "Ken, you are a great leader in the making, but unless you learn to be under authority regardless of the leader above you, you will struggle to be in authority when the time comes."

Those words stung and have echoed in my heart and spirit for years.

I went to the pastor and apologized for my foolishness and we are now great friends. To this day I hold that as one of the principles of my life and ministry. I had learnt a tough life lesson in my village. Learn to be under authority regardless of how great or better you think you are.

We have a proverb in my language (Gikuyu): "An old man sitting on a stool can see farther than a young man who has climbed a tree." I was the young foolish man who had climbed the tree and thought I could see farther than everyone else including those above me. Yet the more I climbed up my tree, the more ignorant I actually looked and the more I exposed my lack of submission.

This lesson was driven home a few years later when I was under a leader whose leadership I really struggled with. He was a great and loveable guy but very segmented and inconsistent in the way he did things. The inconsistencies in vision, strategy and day-to-day operation started to bring tensions within the team.

The team became disconnected and uninterested and slowly started to fall apart. Almost every meeting was a complaining meeting. Unfortunately the leader wasn't there; I was in charge. I tried my best to keep the team together and focused on what needed to be done, but tension was building up and I could see a major implosion on the horizon.

Many joined the team and left either in anger or disappointment because of the leadership style. When asked why I did not leave even when I got better offers from other churches, or was told that others felt I could do things better, I was clear in my heart that this was the leader I was to serve under and support until I felt that the Lord was leading me somewhere else. So I stayed for three years.

We had a great time doing great things for the kingdom. I learnt so much from him, one key thing being how to work both in detailed and big picture mode, something that would pay off a few years later. Nonetheless, we also had very tough seasons where I sometimes felt like quitting or taking up a different role, especially when other offers started looking really tempting.

I had learnt my lesson about submitting to authority even when it causes pain. As long as the core focus of what we did was the cross, I would stay and be under authority and serve as one "serving the Lord, not people" (Eph 6:7).

Many leaders never learn this lesson in their village and it continues to haunt them for years to come. They struggle to accept being under any authority, and thus they either end up splitting churches or planting independent churches in rebellion against authority. Unfortunately I have often seen such churches being unhealthy and giving birth to more church splits. This is a plague on our beautiful continent – church splits, mini-denominations and church plantings born of rebellion.

Even more dangerous, this unhealthy desire not to submit to any authority has given birth to a new generation of lone ranger ministers who do not submit to anyone. In an effort to prevent any possibility of rebellion, they run their churches as a one-man show, controlling them with an iron fist.

These self-appointed bishops, prophets and apostles of our time, are setting a dangerous trend and if not called to order they will bring great shame to the name of Christ and hurt many along the way.

At the beginning it may look all flashy when you are the big one at the top and leading alone, but tough times will come and that is when you will need people who are ahead of you to stand with you.

As I said before, God has no lone rangers nor does he have or need any village heroes. We are part of the body and the Head is Christ Jesus, and he alone has supremacy (Col 1:15–20). You are either submitted to him though the leadership he has established in your life or you are setting yourself up for a great fall.

4

BATTLING GOLIATH

After David had served the king for some time he went back to tending his father's sheep. Then war broke out with the Philistines and Jesse's sons followed Saul into battle (1 Sam 17:13). David, however, is sent to the battlefield only to take food to his brothers and bring back a report to his father (1 Sam 17:17). (Remember, David is still God's anointed king over Israel.)

Then David meets Goliath, the Philistine "champion". As such, he was the nation's "middleman" or fighting representative. He alone fought the middlemen from other nations, and so far no one had defeated him. The Philistines ruled through the victories of their great champion.

To be the nation's representative you had to be able to defeat everybody else in the army, so no doubt this guy was no pushover.

I remember watching the television series *Shaka Zulu* on the life of the great Zulu king and warrior. At that time it was common practice to have the two greatest and fiercest warriors from different tribes battle it out. The winner would not only win the fight for himself; his entire village would be considered victorious.

In one of the episodes Shaka became fed up with this type of warfare and charged across the battlefield to take on the other soldiers. His warriors and the others on the battlefield were confused by this departure from normal practice. But this was the beginning of a new fighting style that led to the rapid expansion of the Zulu kingdom.

Apart from learning to be under authority; it is in our village that we must face the Goliaths of our lives surrounded by those who are close to us, friends and family, where there is support.

Ronald Cottle puts it beautifully: "Fight your foe while you are still surrounded by your family in Christ."[1]

It is sad to see "men and women of God" get embarrassed in public as they battle the Goliath of their life. They are forced to deal with things in full view of the public that they could have dealt with in the privacy of their village.

The examples are endless and known to us; some are within our local churches, others are in the national and even international media.

Every one of us at one point or another will have to stand and face our Goliath.

The moment you decide to step out of the crowd and follow Christ not only as a disciple but to publicly declare the message of the cross, you enter a battle zone. There you will meet your Goliath who hates everything you love and is determined to ensure that you do not achieve anything of significance in the kingdom.

We all have different Goliaths: some struggle with pride, love for money, lust, women, men, greed, fear, low self-esteem, self-righteousness – the list goes on. I am sure we all can put a finger on something we struggle with.

Whatever it is, you need to face it at some point.

It is paramount that you fight this battle while in your early stages of ministry, in your village, surrounded by people who know you authentically, where you can be challenged, wounded, or even struck, but can fall into the loving arms of family.

If you do not fight this battle in your village you will have to fight it later in life when the stakes are higher. There is no avoiding such battles. If you fail then, you will be embarrassed, your immediate family will be devastated, those that you lead will be broken, and the many lives you have touched or influenced for Christ will be shattered.

When it comes to fighting these battles, there are two things that I learnt in my village. The first is that we must learn to focus on God and not on our ability.

In 1 Samuel 17:33, Saul made a mistake that was similar to Samuel's earlier one: he looked at the external issues. David was not a fighter, and had no history as a soldier. When Saul looked at him, he saw a young

---

[1] Cottle, *Anointed to Reign*, 16.

boy who could not do much. And when he looked at Goliath, he saw a ruthless giant who was more than willing to behead anyone.

The stakes were very high; a loss would mean that the entire nation would be subject to Philistine domination (1 Sam 17:8–10).

As you face the Goliaths in your life, do not underestimate or overestimate your ability. David acknowledged that it was God who would deliver him from the hands of the Philistine. Where did David learn this? It must have been one of the lessons he learnt when looking after his father's sheep in his village (1 Sam 17:34–37).

Remember we all have a place of beginning and every lesson we learn in our leadership journey counts for something and God will use it.

It was in the serene mountainsides of Bethlehem that David saw God deliver him from a lion and a bear. He realized that he had not overcome them by his own power but that God had made it possible. So when talking to Saul David continually uses the phrase, "the Lord who delivered me from this and that will deliver me".

God through various circumstances had developed David to a place where he totally depended on him. While the other soldiers saw how big Goliath was (1 Sam 17:11), David saw the greatness and faithfulness of God. While the soldiers remembered the fighting history of Goliath (a warrior from his youth) and the stories they had heard about his ruthlessness with his enemies, David recalled God's faithfulness when he faced the lion and the bear.

We need to look at the various things we face in our lives as pastors. These include pride, sexual sins, habitual sins and many more. Some pastors are so ashamed and afraid of fear of failure or discovery that they decide just to let the current carry them on. But what you need to do is to remember the different situations you have been in and how God rescued you. If he did it then, he will do it again.

One of the strangest encounters I have had was with a church leader who struggled with a smoking addiction that had begun before he came to Christ. In his culture, smoking is considered a sin. When he became a believer, those around him knew that he was a smoker and they walked with him in his recovery journey. But he found that he could not give it up! Eventually he gave up even trying to stop smoking and moved to the city.

As every good believer does, he found a church and connected with it. Soon he was serving there, but no one knew he had a nicotine addiction and that he would often sneak out to take a puff. He never told anyone what was going. He was too embarrassed and the church he was in now was big.

Because of his charismatic leadership, he was soon leading a small group and later overseeing a number of leaders. Then one day during a wedding he sneaked out to take a puff. But this time a member of the church saw him. At first, she could not believe her eyes! She confronted him and later brought the matter to the leadership of the church. The small groups were devastated and the leaders he was mentoring were broken.

He had not dealt with this battle in his village surrounded by people who knew him before salvation, he was now in a big church, leading leaders, where the people only knew him as a key church leader, they did not know about his past battles.

Fight your Goliaths in the village or be ready to face them when you are higher up the leadership ladder and the stakes are far greater.

Remember that we all who are now children of God were sinners at one point and are now children of God by grace alone (Rom 5:8).

God's love for you is unconditional and he is more concerned about your soul than your leadership position or fame in ministry. So as you fight your Goliaths, focus on the fact that God loves you unconditionally and there is no sin so great that he cannot forgive it.

> If we confess our sins, he is faithful and just and will forgive us
> our sins and purify us from all unrighteousness. (1 John 1:9)

When I started leading, I was very scared. Many times I thought I had made a mistake accepting the request to lead. But with time I slowly learnt to focus on God and not on my ability.

The second thing I learnt was to fight the battle God's way and not my way or other people's way. Though Satan our enemy remains the same, every battle is different and our experiences on the battlefield are vast and varied.

It was in the quiet hills of Bethlehem that God taught David the lesson that he must fight all his battles God's way.

Saul lovingly offered his amour to David, and David took it. But the Bible says that when he put it on, he found he could not use it (1 Sam 17:38–39). So he went and got what he was used to and familiar with – a sling and stones.

I'm sure all the military men on the battlefield though this was outrageous. How could this foolish boy go against the well-armoured giant with just stones? Even Goliath was offended when he saw David approaching him (1 Sam 17:42–43).

Imagine the murmuring, astonishment and hushed voices that greeted David as he walked onto the battlefield without armour and without a weapon (as they saw it).

Look at Joshua when he faced Jericho in Joshua 6. This was a fortified city with high, thick walls. God told Joshua to march around the city in silence for seven days and on the seventh day to march around it seven times and then blow the trumpets.

Imagine the generals and soldiers watching these foolish people marching around the walls in silence. They must have laughed, secure inside their big walls. Can you imagine the expressions on the faces of the soldiers of Jericho when the trumpets blasted and the walls came down?

Remember Moses when he stood with Pharaoh's army behind him, the Red Sea in front of him, the people murmuring and crying out as they saw and heard the chariots closing in on them (Exod 14:10). Moses had learnt well in his village (the desert) to trust the God of the impossible. He stretched his rod out over the sea and it parted. If God had told Moses to do this before the encounter at the burning bush, imagine what would have happened!

Look at Christ. To save humanity, he had to die; to make us rich, he became poor; to give us health, he took our sicknesses (2 Cor 8:9; Isa 53:5). He was fighting God's way.

Back to David: He approached Goliath just as God had taught him. When he had faced the lion and bear, he had no armour; it was God who gave him the power to overcome them and save the sheep from the lion's mouth. The same would be true with Goliath. David did not leave home to come and fight Goliath, and he knew that it was not his weapons that would give him victory. Goliath's size did not matter. What was important was the principle: God is faithful.

God was faithful then, and he will be faithful now. David had faith in God and trusted that he would not be put to shame! And God was faithful to his word.

David wrote a lot about this in the psalms. There he constantly talks about God being his shield and defence, his fortress, his protection and much more (see, for example, Ps 18:2). He was putting into words the lessons that had begun in Bethlehem.

Do not put any confidence in your ability to overcome troubles. Have faith in God that he will give you victory over your Goliath. We need to remember that "the weapons we fight with are not the weapons of the world. On the contrary, they have divine power to demolish strongholds" (2 Cor 10:4).

You can learn principles and strategies from great servants of God, you can read them in great books, but you must learn to fight the battle of faith for yourself, fully trusting in God alone. No one else can fight this battle for you. The more you postpone these battles, the harder it is to confront them once you start going up the ladder.

My heart was so broken when I first learnt of a wonderful pastor who was caught up in sexual sin. This was a guy I knew and admired. As the details started to come out, I learnt that this was not the first time this had happened. Earlier in his ministry life, when he was still a volunteer, he had had sexual relations with another volunteer. But to keep appearances up, the church he was serving in swept these matters under the carpet and asked him to leave.

He kept on struggling with this aspect of his life and never sought help or someone to talk to. Now the same sin had caught up with him again. Only this time he was a pastor, married to a wonderful lady, and they had a child.

The cost of postponing foundational battles is just too high!

Know what areas you struggle with and fight those battles early in your leadership journey. The shame brought to the cross and the work of ministry is far too high if you fail to do so. Your church will pay the price.

One major battle I had to fight early in leading my new church was my own fear. As I stepped into leadership, I was very scared of failing. I was now responsible for an entire congregation, the preaching, finances, building a team and growing the church.

In panic I started reading all the books I could get on leadership. I asked around about what was the latest book on one thing or the other. However, some of these books did more harm than good. They made me even more scared when I read how easily the pastors in those books seemed to have grown their ministries while I was struggling.

In one book on team-building, the author talked about hiring the best people money can buy. At that point our budget was in the red. I remember feeling a sense of despair. How was I ever going to get good people without money?

My focus had totally shifted from looking to the Lord for provision. I also shifted focus from spending time praying for good workers to thinking about where I could get money to hire the best people.

I constantly asked what I was doing wrong. I was trying to fight my battle in someone else's armour.

Then like the prodigal son in Luke 15:17, I "came to my senses". I reflected on all the victories God had given me when I was leading the youth ministry way back in my village and in the city. I had been preaching, running a small budget, building a team with no money – the same things I was now required to do but on a bigger scale. If God saw me through then, he would be able to see me through this new role.

5

PROTECTING YOUR ACHILLES' HEEL

In Greek mythology there is an individual known as Achilles, who was one of the bravest and greatest warriors of his time. He was greater than mortal man but was not quite a god.

It is said that when Achilles was a baby, his mother dipped him in the River Styx in order to make him immortal. Achilles became invulnerable except for the heel by which she had held him. He won many victories, but during one major battle he was struck by an arrow on his heel and died.

The metaphor of an Achilles' heel has endured for centuries and is used to refer to flaws or gaps in our lives that permit the tip of an arrow to penetrate where we are most vulnerable. It turns out that many individuals in the Bible had this type of flaw, and chances are that most of us do too.

I cannot overemphasize the fact that our world is full of men, women, presidents, doctors, lawyers, politicians, pastors, priests and many more who have risen to great heights in their careers, but who suddenly fall in the middle of a moral, spiritual or emotional battle. This fall seems to come from nowhere, and is catastrophic.

Somehow in the church we have not yet got used to it, and it seems to shock us each time.

There was a pastor who was caught with his hands in the church building kitty. After investigation it is discovered he had being defrauding the church for a few years. The church was traumatized. The board fired the pastor, but as part of restoration they also required him to go through counselling. He moved on. Because he was a brilliant leader and preacher, he was able to find another pastoral position in another town.

Two years later he was caught in the same situation, with his hands in the kitty.

Until that pastor realizes that his love of money is his Achilles' heel, repents, and asks fellow ministers to walk with him, this cycle will keep repeating itself and more churches and lives will be broken everywhere he goes.

Your Achilles' heel is one of the greatest enemies to your spiritual and emotional growth as a leader. It will ensure you are spiritually and emotionally stifled, no matter how charismatic or inspirational a leader you are.

Some people believe the fallacy that your life can be divided into two parts: "my walk with God" part and "my personal life". They think that what happens in their private or personal life is their business and what happens in their Christian life is their business with God. This lie has somehow gripped many young African pastors who are copying everything from the West without question. The premise that if it's on TV or in a book and it's from the West then it is true is the undoing of many.

Because of our elevated positions in society, many pastors like me are too scared to let anyone know that we have flaws and need help. Our congregations and the external images many of us have created have become more important to us than the salvation of our souls from the sins that so easily entangle us.

Before you are a mighty man of God, you are just a man prone to the challenges and temptations of life. You are not indestructible.

An Ashanti proverb says "no one tests the depth of a river with both feet". Only a fool would do that! Yet this is what we do every time we get into ministry and think that it is a personal decision. We may even believe that because we are pastors we are immune to the attacks of the enemy. But when you step up to lead in God's kingdom you step into the limelight and everyone can see you. You become an easy target for anyone throwing things.

Every leader, and especially pastors, must reflect on the warning in 1 Peter 5:8: "Be alert and of sober mind. Your enemy the devil prowls around like a roaring lion looking for someone to devour."

This is a cardinal truth. Brothers and sisters, we are in a war, and this war is for your soul! Scripture informs us that this war is "not against flesh and blood, but against … the powers of this dark world and against the spiritual forces of evil in the heavenly realms" (Eph 6:10).

Your spiritual growth as a leader is a defeat to the kingdom of darkness. Thus Satan will not sit around and let you grow, because he knows that as you grow he loses ground. And like any enemy he will not attack you in your areas of strength; no, he will attack you where you are most vulnerable, your Achilles' heel.

Reflecting on the battle between David and Goliath we see great truths.

David was not only fighting a physical battle but also a spiritual one. Depending on how the battle would end, there were going to be both spiritual and physical implications. The spiritual implications would be that by losing to Goliath, David would send the whole nation into political bondage and slavery. For Israel, the covenant nation, this would be a devastating blow. This is what King Saul did not understand. He was fixated on the physical aspect of the battle. He kept looking at Goliath's size and comparing it to the size of his biggest warrior and losing hope. His fixation on the physical aspect of battle is captured in his speech to his men in 1 Samuel 17:24–33.

But David realized what was going on was something more than just a physical battle. We can hear his insight into the spiritual battle as we listen to what he said as he approached Goliath:

> David said to the Philistine, "You come against me with sword and spear and javelin, but I come against you in the name of the Lord Almighty, the God of the armies of Israel, whom you have defied. This day the Lord will deliver you into my hands, and I'll strike you down and cut off your head. This very day I will give the carcasses of the Philistine army to the birds and the wild animals, and the whole world will know that there is a God in Israel. All those gathered here will know that it is not by sword or spear that the Lord saves; for the battle is the

Lord's, and he will give all of you into our hands." (1 Sam 17:45–47)

Doesn't this sound similar to Ephesians 6:10–13?

> Finally, be strong in the Lord and in his mighty power. Put on the full armour of God, so that you can take your stand against the devil's schemes. For our struggle is not against flesh and blood, but against the rulers, against the authorities, against the powers of this dark world and against the spiritual forces of evil in the heavenly realms. Therefore put on the full armour of God, so that when the day of evil comes, you may be able to stand your ground, and after you have done everything, to stand.

Every road to spiritual growth includes a spiritual battlefield, and in every battlefield there is a Goliath, pridefully challenging you to a fight, attacking you where you are most vulnerable.

These Goliaths, as I mentioned earlier, may be issues with anger, inability to manage time or money, jealousy, the beginnings of an addiction, low self-esteem, pride, arrogance, inability to set boundaries, lust and many more. These are our battlefields and these are our enemies. You can either look at them from Saul's point of view and see them as merely physical struggles around "my issues" and choose to ignore them, or you can look at them from David's point of view and recognize that these are spiritual battles for your own soul and for your ministry.

If Satan can succeed in convincing you that these battles are private and have no implications for your spiritual leadership, then he has already won half the battle. The truth is your spiritual growth as a leader will be hindered, stifled and even killed by the things going on in your private world. And your fall will be public, not private. Moreover, as long as you don't deal with things like unhealthy anger as a leader, you will find that you don't experience the joy that is a fruit of the Spirit. Your relationships will always be in unhealthy tension. Your inability to set good boundaries will affect your personal Bible study and devotion time and lead you down a path of spiritual dryness. Your pride and arrogance will rob you of the growth brought about by being part of the body of Christ.

Regardless of how many routes you take to avoid the battlefield where you have to deal with your vulnerabilities, you will find yourself there at some point or another, face-to-face with Goliath, simply because the devil does not take a break. From the day you decided to follow Christ, and even more so from the day you stepped into the ministry arena, you have entered into battle and there is no neutral ground, there is no "private space".

As a leader you need to know your weaknesses and bring them to the Lord in prayer. As the Holy Spirit convicts you of these matters, lay them bare at the foot of the cross. And then find fellow believers you can trust to walk with you though this battle and to accompany you on your ministry journey. The companionship of such believers is one of the joys of being part of the body of Christ.

Hebrews 12:1 tells us, "Therefore, since we are surrounded by such a great cloud of witnesses, let us throw off everything that hinders and the sin that so easily entangles. And let us run with perseverance the race marked out for us." This is part of leadership growth, continually throwing off and dropping weights that entangle us and make the race of faith hard and difficult to focus on.

When we read 1 Samuel 17 about how David, against all odds, defeated Goliath, we are filled with excitement. What many do not remember is that before he was propelled onto the national stage fighting for king and country, he won little victories in his Bethlehem.

When he killed the bear and lions, maybe only his parents, brothers and village friends knew about it. But eventually he would face and defeat Goliath in front of two nations and his king.

Know what your areas of vulnerability are and work on them while you are still in the safety of familiar surroundings.

6

IN RHYTHM WITH GOD

The leadership we are called to by Christ is of an extremely high standard, for we deal with matters that have eternal consequences. As we engage in mission and outreach, people will hear the gospel and consider making a decision to follow Christ. Their decisions will change their destinies eternally.

In saying this, I am not dismissing the importance of other professions and leadership roles. But I know that what I have been entrusted with is of such great value and weight that compromise on my part is not an option. We are told, "We are therefore Christ's ambassadors, as though God were making his appeal through us" (2 Cor 5:20). Though the weight of this responsibility is heavy and the expectations high, God has promised that he will never leave or forsake me and even in the hardest of times I can still trust in him because he is dependable.

I have a friend who is the CEO of a corporation. His lifestyle inspires me. He is in the gym at 5.30 a.m. for an hour and a half, then he heads home to have breakfast with his kids before they go to school, he then jumps into the job of leading a fast growing financial company. Over weekends, he plays golf with clients and potential clients or chairs high-powered board meetings.

He doesn't strike me as the gym type or as someone who is particularly interested in looking muscular, so I asked him why he kept going to the gym. He told me that if he is not in good physical and mental shape, it has a direct impact on his output at work. Going to the gym helps him keep on top of things and in balance, not to competition standards but in the business world.

As I reflected on what he had said, I was convicted about how physically unfit I was and I took up cycling. But what I also saw was how seemingly unrelated parts of a person's life are connected and can have a direct impact on each other.

My mind raced on to the last part of Philippians 2:12: "continue to work out your salvation with fear and trembling." How great a need this is among pastors and church leaders!

Many pastors, myself included, quote this verse when encouraging, rebuking or inspiring others but rarely do we see it as a polished mirror reflecting back to us that as we speak to others, we also speak to ourselves.

As pastors and leaders we need to know that the way you lead you own self will be reflected in the way you lead others. The need for good spiritual health and a balanced life is both foundational and paramount. You cannot downplay the essential need for a healthy spiritual life if you are going to lead because there is nothing as dangerous as a lukewarm spiritual leader. Revelation 3:16 says, "because you are lukewarm – neither hot nor cold – I am about to spit you out of my mouth".

Taking a cue from my CEO friend, if you are not spiritually fit on a personal level as a leader it will have direct impact on your ability to lead in the kingdom. Once you start to die spiritually, your ministry also starts to die. You can fake it, ignore it, or run on the fuel of the past, but at some point you will reach your breaking point.

The Apostle Paul writes to Timothy, "For physical training is of some value, but godliness has value for all things, holding promise for both the present life and the life to come" (1 Tim 4:8).

I learnt this lesson the hard way, and since then I have made a decision: I will not lose the joy my salvation for the "glory" of a successful ministry.

What I am about to say may sound absurd, but it is very true: You can be so out of touch with Christ that you don't realize that you long ago stopped being his disciple.

You may have a very successful ministry, but I have come to learn that my own spiritual health and my faithfulness to the one who called me is a matter of life and death, and I mean eternal life and eternal death.

Don't be surprised to meet pastors who don't pray, who cannot tell you the last time they read their Bible not for sermon preparation but for personal growth. You will find pastors who cannot remember the last time they fasted not because of the financial situation of the church or because a key worship leader had left but because they wanted to be aligned with the Master.

I reached a point in my early years of leadership where I was reading more leadership books than the Bible. I was spending more time strategizing for ministry growth than praying for the harvest. I was spending more time building networks than building that which mattered most – my inner man.

One day I went for a personal retreat, to strategize some more. I sat on a bench in the beautiful, cool garden of a secluded Catholic retreat centre and began to read a leadership book. I took copious notes. Lying next to me was my Bible, which I did not even open. I outlined all the things that needed to change at church and the strategic discussions I needed to have with different people. All these were good thoughts, and my time I thought was well spent, but I was missing the main thing.

As I continued to read and take notes, I glanced over at my Bible. Something in me broke and tears started rolling down my cheeks. It hit me! I had replaced the truth with a lie! I felt the weight of Peter's statement echo in my heart "Lord, to whom shall we go? You have the words of eternal life" (John 6:68).

I had left the words of eternal life and in my desperate search for answers to the problems of leadership I had gone after earthly wisdom. I was no longer praying because I had all these great books to read. I was totally out of rhythm with God and was ready to make music on my own. I was a leader living and now almost leading on empty!

Oh how foolish I was!

In that instant I learnt a life lesson: my spiritual health as a child of God is more important than the size of my ministry!

Once you are out of rhythm with God, you dance to your own beat. You create your own music and set the tempo … you add the notes you like and remove the ones you don't. But when the music stops, you realize that all that you have put together is not a beautiful song but a compilation of dreadful sounds from a broken and sinful heart.

To be in rhythm with God is to come to a place of total surrender and to acknowledge that God holds the master score sheet on which we are only small musical notes. By ourselves we cannot make beautiful music. By focusing on things other than the Master Conductor who is Jesus, we go off beat, off tempo, and the whole orchestra sounds bad.

We must remember that "it is God who works in you to will and to act in order to fulfil his good purpose" (Phil 2:13). The Apostle Paul understood this very well. In 1 Timothy 2:3–7 he says:

> This is good, and pleases God our Saviour, who wants all people to be saved and to come to a knowledge of the truth. For there is one God and one mediator between God and mankind, the man Christ Jesus, who gave himself as a ransom for all people. This has now been witnessed to at the proper time. And for this purpose I was appointed a herald and an apostle – I am telling the truth, I am not lying – and a true and faithful teacher of the Gentiles. (1 Tim 2:3–7)

Paul acknowledges that the origin of our mission to see people come to Jesus started with God. We were never the originators; we are just entrusted with ministry. Secondly, he acknowledges that this mission objective is accomplished only through Jesus' death on the cross. It is from this point of understanding that Paul sees his ministry and calling as both a herald and an apostle.

When we as leaders see ministry in the same way as Paul saw it, we recognize that we are responsible to be disciples before we are leaders. The more you allow self and other things to grow, the more likely you are to take your focus off God and see yourself as important. In this prideful state we will produce nothing but noise! Like John the Baptist in John 3:30 we must proclaim every day, "He must become greater; I must become less."

Only God in his sovereignty has the ability to put together our brokenness and use it to write beautiful songs. We need to be in rhythm with his song; it doesn't work the other way round.

Always remember before you and I ever existed, God loved the world.

From the day I had that insight in the garden, I have changed a few things. Now when I go on retreat I deliberately take only one leadership book, or just a printout of a few chapters. I spend most of the time praying for various things, and especially for the harvest; I rest and immerse myself in personal devotion on areas I am struggling with.

So if I know I am starting to exhibit unhealthy anger at work, I will use my time on the retreat to pray thoroughly about that issue, mostly repenting. I will study God's word on anger and its consequences with a desire to get back in rhythm with God.

7

IN THE INNER CHAMBERS

Knowing that you need to take responsibility for your spiritual growth is one thing, actually doing it is another.

Have you ever had the experience of your phone's battery running out of charge during the day? Have you ever remembered to connect your phone to the charging unit at night, and then woken up to discover that either you had not switched on the power at the socket or had not connected the cables properly so that your phone had not charged? We all know how frustrating that is! We live in a fast world, where everything is travelling at the speed of light. The mobile phone has revolutionized Kenya, the African continent and the world at large in less than two decades. Life has become impossible without one.

But when I was dating, we did not have mobile phones. So I would have to stand in line at a phone booth, and when my turn eventually came I would call my fiancée and talk until I ran out of coins to keep the connection going. I knew by heart the phone numbers of a number of phone booths outside particular buildings, and I would call her from there or would ask her to call me at that booth at a particular time. Often I wasn't the only guy waiting there for a call.

I remember that when I was growing up I and the other boys thought that the path to high esteem was to become a safari rally driver. So we used to make wire cars and race them around the village. We had no TV in our homes in those days, and in the evenings we would sit around the fire and sing as our grandfather repeated the same story for us, varying the ending depending on how much he had had to drink that night.

These days, by contrast, even young children can recite mobile phone numbers from memory. My daughter at only two and a half could operate my iPad. I have had to put in a passcode to stop her from buying all the dress-up games in the iTunes store! When I go to my village, I even see old men and women using mobile phones.

The mobile phone has become such a part of our life that if you meet someone who has lost their phone it's as if they have been bereaved; they almost want to hold a funeral service.

This technological revolution has redefined community, reshaped relationships and opened the world to a new frontier. It has also given people access to you 24/7; you cannot hide! People text you and want instant replies to questions you need time to think about. And if you don't reply at once, they call you to ask if you got their urgent text message.

It's not just mobile phones. Life as a whole has become busier and busier. People are working hard. Social pressure and ambition push us so hard that to remain relevant, you have to change as fast as the world is changing. It is like you are constantly on the highway with no time to stop for petrol.

It is not uncommon to find someone with an 8 to 5 job who leaves the office and goes to class from 6 p.m. to 9 p.m. Then they go home and do assignments until 1 a.m. and the cycle starts all over again. I once met a woman who was a student at the main campus but was also attending three other colleges, one for accounting, another for management, and a third for something else, all at the same time! And she was only 21! The days when a diploma was able to get you somewhere in the African economy are fading fast.

As we are all caught up in this ever-changing life race, some things remain the same; we are still pastors and leaders, and God has called us to shepherd these very busy people and, above all, to live a life worthy of our calling.

In my quest for self-leadership, I became aware of the need to have an inner chamber, a place of slowing down, resting and reflecting, a place where I can listen to the still, small voice. This insight came to me during a time I went through what I call an Elijah encounter. I got that name for them from the experiences of Elijah in 1 Kings 18 and 19.

Elijah had endured some tough years. He had been hiding from King Ahab, who wanted him dead. So for some time he had stayed outside the country. Then he had the great encounter at Mount Carmel and came out on top. He engaged Baal's prophets in a whole day event which culminated in mass murder of the false prophets and the restoration of the nation to the worship of the one true God.

> At the time of sacrifice, the prophet Elijah stepped forward and prayed: "LORD, the God of Abraham, Isaac and Israel, let it be known today that you are God in Israel and that I am your servant and have done all these things at your command. Answer me, LORD, answer me, so these people will know that you, LORD, are God, and that you are turning their hearts back again."
>
> Then the fire of the LORD fell and burned up the sacrifice, the wood, the stones and the soil, and also licked up the water in the trench.
>
> When all the people saw this, they fell prostrate and cried, "The LORD – he is God! The LORD – he is God!"
>
> Then Elijah commanded them, "Seize the prophets of Baal. Don't let anyone get away!" They seized them, and Elijah had them brought down to the Kishon Valley and slaughtered there. (1 Kgs 18:36–40)

But when Queen Jezebel retaliated and threatened him, Elijah ran for his life. He travelled about a hundred miles from Jezreel down to Beersheba, located along the outer border of Israel (that's quite a few days journey). There he left his servant behind and went on one day's journey into the desert.

This brother was tired. He was so fed up with life that he became suicidal; he wanted to just lie there and die.

> Now Ahab told Jezebel everything Elijah had done and how he had killed all the prophets with the sword. So Jezebel sent a messenger to Elijah to say, "May the gods deal with me, be it ever so severely, if by this time tomorrow I do not make your life like that of one of them."
>
> Elijah was afraid and ran for his life. When he came to Beersheba in Judah, he left his servant there, while he himself went a day's journey into the wilderness. He came to a broom bush, sat down under it and prayed that he might die. "I have

had enough, LORD," he said. "Take my life; I am no better than my ancestors." (1 Kgs 19:1–4)

I have been at that point (not suicidal) but on the verge of giving up because I was tired, worn out, and slipping into the "I just don't care" mode. And I have met a number of pastors in the same position. They are tired and worn out; the ever-increasing pace of life has pounded them into the corner of submission.

That's the way we are sometimes, we keep going and going and going like the rabbit in the Energizer Bunny commercial and eventually we run dry and stall.

We are literary running after the sheep we shepherd, and they keep inventing new ways of being busy, and so we up our tempo.

People need to get to work early, so we introduce morning services. They can't read their Bible consistently, so we introduce apps to keep them reading or send a devotion via text message. All these inventions are driven and sustained by people like you and me. We now have to prepare a sermon for the "morning glory" service from Monday to Friday, and prepare short daily devotionals for the Bible app or text message, and so on. And I haven't even mentioned blog posts and websites yet!

We used to preach only once or maybe twice on Sunday; now we have to preach at six more services. If we add in writing a daily devotional, that is twelve more messages we now have to prepare. Our entire week can be consumed with writing and preparing messages, inventing new ways of casting the net wider and farther.

But like everything else created by God, you and I need to rest and rejuvenate. When we don't, we burn out and burnout is a ministry killer. It brings us to the point where we start to let go and not care anymore.

Do you really think God needs to rest? He is all-powerful, more than able, I mean he rules over the universe and all the hosts of heaven. He knows what the birds of the air need and they are never without food. Yet God took time to rest.

> Thus the heavens and the earth were completed in all their vast array.
>
> By the seventh day God had finished the work he had been doing; so on the seventh day he rested from all his work. Then

> God blessed the seventh day and made it holy, because on it he rested from all the work of creating that he had done. (Gen 2:1–4)

In the Ten Commandments, the commandment about the Sabbath is the only one in which the word "holy" is used.

> Remember the Sabbath day by keeping it holy. Six days you shall labour and do all your work, but the seventh day is a sabbath to the LORD your God. On it you shall not do any work, neither you, nor your son or daughter, nor your male or female servant, nor your animals, nor any foreigner residing in your towns. For in six days the LORD made the heavens and the earth, the sea, and all that is in them, but he rested on the seventh day. Therefore the LORD blessed the Sabbath day and made it holy. (Exod 20:8–11)

God was teaching us a principle both at creation and in the Ten Commandments. He did not create our body to run on solar or lithium batteries; he created us to need rest. He modelled how significant this was by taking time to rest.

We must understand that there comes a time when we need to disconnect from the world and just REST. Take time away and just slow down, unwind and go to the inner chamber.

I really struggled with the concept of rest, I justified my thinking by stating that the world is dying and people need to hear about Jesus, I will rest when I get to heaven … I know I'm not alone in this pattern of thinking.

I learnt the secret of the inner chamber from a great mentor, Pastor Muriithi Wanjau of Mavuno Church. He was always going on retreat for one reason or another. He was either on a prayer retreat, a resting retreat, a thinking retreat – you name it he had a retreat for it.

When I was asked to lead, one of the things Pastor Oscar put on the table as a non-negotiable was that I was to meet with Pastor Muriithi at least twice a month. We ended up meeting every Friday for a year. During those meetings Pastor Muriithi taught me the importance of resting and retreating. He was leading a big church, with numbers in the thousands, and yet he found time to retreat. I was leading a church of about a hundred and twenty people, and felt I was too busy to retreat and rest. I would be so consumed with work that my Monday rest day became an excuse to get more done.

Pastor Muriithi would always ask me to schedule rest and reflection time and to learn to jealously guard my day off. He realized that rest was not something I did naturally hence the need to schedule it.

When we don't rest or create an inner chamber, we begin to lose focus on what really matters. We forget the core of why we responded to the call to serve. We shift the focus from the Great Commission and the Master to ourselves, our needs and our wants.

The same thing happened to Elijah: Because of the situation that surrounded him he lost focus on what really mattered.

This is the same prophet who had raised dead people!

> Then he cried out to the LORD, "LORD my God, have you brought tragedy even on this widow I am staying with, by causing her son to die?" Then he stretched himself out on the boy three times and cried out to the LORD, "LORD my God, let this boy's life return to him!"
>
> The LORD heard Elijah's cry, and the boy's life returned to him, and he lived. Elijah picked up the child and carried him down from the room into the house. He gave him to his mother and said, "Look, your son is alive!" (1 Kgs 17:20–23)

This is the same prophet who had called fire from heaven, and who had said that his word had said there would be no rain or dew for 3 years.

> Now Elijah the Tishbite, from Tishbe in Gilead, said to Ahab, "As the LORD, the God of Israel, lives, whom I serve, there will be neither dew nor rain in the next few years except at my word." (1 Kgs 17:1)

Now all Elijah did was to complain to God that he was the only one left, all the other prophets had been killed, and now they even wanted to kill him.

Because of being so caught up in things he had lost his focus on the big picture and the amazing miracle that had taken place on Mount Carmel – the restoration of a nation by a covenant-keeping God.

> When all the people saw this, they fell prostrate and cried, "The
> LORD – he is God! The LORD – he is God!" (1 Kgs 18:39)

Lack of rest leads us to lose focus on the bigger picture.

We are so busy doing this and that before moving on to the next thing that we sometimes do not take time to refocus on where we are headed or on the people and things that really matter.

Elijah had done the same. At one point he was leading the nation towards restoration, but somewhere he lost focus and it became about him, who did what and why.

Elijah is referred to as the prophet of fire. So it is interesting that in 1 Kings 19 God chooses to use a gentle whisper rather than fire, wind and earthquake to teach Elijah something. A whisper portrays a sense of calmness, collectedness, peace and restfulness.

But God also showed his might to Elijah in the wind, fire and earthquake. God reminded him that he was still the God who answers by fire and is more than able.

When we rest we are able to take time to refocus on what really matters, our inner being.

God reminded Elijah that it was not all about him but about the children of Israel. God told him that there were as many as 7000 who had not bowed to the god Baal. Despite the persecution by Jezebel, three years of drought and hiding in caves, they had held onto their faith (1 Kgs 19:18). Those were the people God was concerned about and they were the reason he had called Elijah.

We chase after the wind and fire and the things that bring earthquakes but the Lord is not only in those things. Rest and take time to refocus of what really matters. Learn the principle of the inner chamber.

I thank the Lord for a great mentor he gave me in Pastor Muriithi. I was headed down a very dangerous path of potential burnout; this principle he taught me has kept me focused.

I cannot overemphasize the importance of learning to retreat into the inner chamber. Don't be caught up in the speed of life. Remain relevant and up to date, but always be anchored on Christ the solid rock.

If you find it hard to slow down, schedule rest into your life. Ask a close friend to hold you accountable to taking time away.

From the outset teach your congregation, no matter how big or small, to honour your time of rest and day off. I once heard a minister say, "You get what you allow". If you teach your congregation that you have no rest time, then you give them permission to call on you all day, every day on all matters. If you teach your congregation to honour your rest time and day off, then they will give you space to rest.

So I learnt how to go on retreat alone, to meditate on God's word, to be still, silent, reflective, to find silence in a noisy world. This has transformed my life, both as a child of God and also in my leadership. It is in these moments of silence and solitude that the Lord has spoken some of the greatest truths to me. He has shone his light on my areas of weakness and spoken affirmation to my areas of strength.

God knows that we are but dust, we grow weak and must rest.

Christ understood this principle very well. At times he just took time away and rested. He did not let anyone disturb him, even when his fame had spread and everyone wanted a piece of him, he still withdrew and rested.

> Yet the news about him spread all the more, so that crowds of people came to hear him and to be healed of their sicknesses. But Jesus often withdrew to lonely places and prayed. (Luke 5:15–16)

Many pastors are guilty of the messiah syndrome, we want to save the world. We are also the ones people call all the time; we marry them, we bury them, we give them counsel, we baptize them, we dedicate their babies, houses and cars, we preach to them, we intercede for them, and the list goes on and on. Your congregation will never have enough of you, that is a fact. This is especially the case when a church is still young and you are the one who has to do everything.

My father in-law, whom I worked under for a while, told me that "one man died for all so that no one else would have to". I don't intend to die by carrying the entire church on my back, because Christ died once and for all, his death was sufficient!

8

FIRST THINGS FIRST

I was once invited to speak at a pastors' leadership conference attended by pastors, bishops and evangelists from rural Kenya and around East Africa. These were men in the front line of ministry in very hard places. Despite facing many challenges, these men had been faithful and committed to seeing the gospel spread.

When they were invited to this conference, the only condition was that they must come with their spouse. I asked why they had this condition. The pastor who was organizing the conference explained that he and others had noticed that many pastors had never had marital counselling or been to a marriage seminar. They also noticed that very few pastors' wives actually attended any leadership conferences, yet they were leaders in their own right.

The pastor said that after noticing this disconnect in the marriages, they developed something to address it. On the last night of the conference, they held a dinner where the men of God were to spend time with their wives and tell them how much they loved them.

It was mind-boggling to learn that some of these ministers had not told their wives "I love you" for a very long time. Some had not even held hands or been intimate with their wives for a long time. At the dinner, some of the wives became emotional, others wore stone cold expressions, still others were extremely guarded, not knowing what to do.

As pastors, we find it very awkward when we are the ones on the other side of the table. Most of the time we are the ones who are invited to speak or facilitate sessions at marriage seminars or conferences. We are the experts. We do the counselling both before and after the wedding.

We are the ones people come to see when things are starting to bud and love is in the air and when a marriage hits rough patches.

In some cultures in Africa, showing emotion to your wife is interpreted as a sign of weakness on the part of the man. But as ministers we are to take the Bible as the finally authority on all matters, even cultural ones, and the Bible is very clear that the expression of love is part of the DNA of the marriage covenant:

> Husbands, love your wives, just as Christ loved the church and gave himself up for her to make her holy, cleansing her by the washing with water through the word, and to present her to himself as a radiant church, without stain or wrinkle or any other blemish, but holy and blameless. In this same way, husbands ought to love their wives as their own bodies. He who loves his wife loves himself. After all, no one ever hated their own body, but they feed and care for their body, just as Christ does the church – for we are members of his body. "For this reason a man will leave his father and mother and be united to his wife, and the two will become one flesh." This is a profound mystery – but I am talking about Christ and the church. However, each one of you also must love his wife as he loves himself, and the wife must respect her husband. (Eph 5:25–33)

Christ loved us and displayed this love by dying on the cross for you and me. This is the message that we as pastors proclaim, but we must also allow it to transform us and saturate every aspect of our lives, including our family and marriage life. Culture should never be used as an excuse to have a terrible marriage or family.

I know a few pastors whose marriages fell apart. They are now divorced. I also know of many other marriages that are in danger as families are slowly breaking apart.

In the competition for a pastor's attention, everything else gets bumped up in the in-tray except the most crucial item, the family. I have learnt over the last few years that as your church grows in number and influence, as you get invited to speak more often, or even just as you work on getting a new church plant off the ground, your family takes the greatest hit. The excuse list for not spending time with your wife and children becomes longer and longer and more legitimate as growth starts to happen.

There is an assumption that the family understands the strains of ministry and hence should give the pastor space to work. But this is a lie from the very pit of hell put out there by the father of all lies, the devil. In reality, your family needs you more than the church does. A church can always get another pastor, a conference can always replace you as the keynote speaker, but your family will always only have you. You cannot delegate your fatherhood responsibilities to your elders or deacons. You cannot even delegate them to your wife!

We were once handling a very complicated and sensitive leadership matter at our church. The situation had the potential of bringing a split among the people we were dealing with. During lengthy discussions on the best way forward, one of the elders told us a story to illustrate his point.

> There were once three cows, black, white and brown. They were very close and a formidable force against the hyena. He could never manage to take them on in his quest for a good lunch. Even when they were not together, they were never far apart, and were always within earshot. The hyena had tried to attack them but was always repelled because they were so strong as a team.
>
> So the hyena devised a plan. In the cool of the day when the other two cows were resting in the shade, he went to the black cow and quickly whispered to him, that they (the hyena and his friends) were planning to attack them in the dark. It was going to be easy because the white cow always gave away their location because of her colour.
>
> The hyena then retreated into the thickets. The black cow was very concerned and whispered the same message to the brown cow. The two of them decided to quietly part ways with the white cow. Alone and confused, the white cow was vulnerable and did not last the night.
>
> A few weeks later the hyena again met the brown cow and said, "You see, the white cow is no more". He then whispered that they were planning another attack and that it was going to

be easy because when they were grazing the black cow did not blend in with the vegetation. Fearing for her life, the brown cow quietly slipped away into the forest. Now both cows were separate and the hyena had an easy time killing them both.

The hyena knew that together these cows were never going to fall, but if he could separate them, half his work was done.

The same is true of pastors and their families. A pastor is vulnerable if his marriage and family are on shaky ground. This is the case when the pastor's children do not feel loved by their father, or his wife sees the church as a threat and as competition to her marriage.

I have learnt the hard way that not everyone who walks into your office does so with good intentions. There are people out there who have knowingly or unknowingly allowed themselves to be used to destroy marriages and families. They take you away from your time at home. They are constantly demanding for more of you. Like the hyena, they slowly separate you from your spouse, and then from your children. Once you are alone and vulnerable, you become easy prey.

As a pastor you are in the crosshairs of the enemy and he will work to bring you down. With a shaky marriage and a breaking family you are like one of the cows alone in the forest against a pack of clever and hungry hyenas.

Scripture is crystal clear: "Be alert and of sober mind. Your enemy the devil prowls around like a roaring lion looking for someone to devour" (1 Pet 5:8). So be alert and make your family your first ministry. After all, this is one of the key requirements for church leadership. A leader must be able to lead at home.

> He must manage his own family well and see that his children obey him, and he must do so in a manner worthy of full respect. (If anyone does not know how to manage his own family, how can he take care of God's church?) (1 Tim 3:4–5)

Shepherding God's flock is a great responsibility, shepherding your family is an even greater one. Don't confuse the two. Your children are not just members of your congregation; they are your children first.

Many pastors will go the extra mile to counsel other people's children, pray for them and invest time in discipling them. But they will shout at their children and not take time to have devotions with their family. In the evening they will claim to be too tired to do so after a hard day's work. But should a church member call in need of help, the pastor will leave the food on the table and go to them.

Pastors will also put pressure on their children to be the perfect pastor's kids, purely for public show – that is the height of pride. These children already carry the label of being the pastor's child. Young as they are, they carry the weight of the expectation that they will be different.

You cannot build the kingdom at the expense of your family. If you do, you will ensure that your spouse and children hate the church and even God for taking you away from them.

As a pastor I know how easy it is do this. People's expectations of us can sometimes be unrealistic, and we stand in the spotlight as our families fade in the background, until soon they become nothing but distant noise.

I have worked hard to let my children know that I love them more than I love the church I lead, not only in words but also in deeds. I have worked hard to ensure that my wife feels free to keep me in check when I start to drift and immerse myself in ministry at the expense of the family. When she does this, the conversation is never easy. I get defensive and try to justify my actions. But at the end of the day I know she is right. She is the only one who sees my major blind spots in the family, and her role is to smack me back into reality.

I often compare the endings of two great men in the Bible. Samuel and Joshua. Both did great things for God and the nation of Israel. Joshua was a leader mentored by Moses. He experienced God's deliverance first-hand and had the privilege of leading the nation into the Promised Land. At the end of this long ministry journey, what counted most for him is captured at the end of Joshua 24:15: "But as for me and my household, we will serve the Lord."

After considering everything pertaining to his leadership journey over a period of eighty years, Joshua's greatest achievement was summed up in this statement. His family's eternal destiny was secure in God. That was what mattered!

Contrast this to the situation of Israel's greatest judge, Samuel, a man who also served God faithfully for many years.

When Samuel grew old, he appointed his sons as Israel's leaders. The name of his firstborn was Joel and the name of his second was Abijah, and they served at Beersheba. But his sons did not follow his ways. They turned aside after dishonest gain and accepted bribes and perverted justice.

So all the elders of Israel gathered together and came to Samuel at Ramah. They said to him, "You are old, and your sons do not follow your ways; now appoint a king to lead us, such as all the other nations have." (1 Sam 8:1–5)

His sons were a great disappointment, and this led to the people rejecting God as their leader and demanding a king. This must have been heartbreaking for Samuel, and it can happen to us too.

We may be great ministers and build great churches but it all counts for nothing if we cannot lead our family. So put first things first. Build your home base; the rest should follow.

9

BOUNDARIES

I remember one time when I was to meet with a certain lady for counselling, I asked her to come to my office, but because of her work schedule she could not make it. So the compromise was to meet at a local coffee shop.

She was there when I arrived. We drank coffee as I listened to her problems. We must have been there for over an hour. As we got up to leave, she mentioned that she had taken a cab to get there and asked me to drop her at her office, which was on my way anyway. I obliged.

We had scheduled to meet in my office the following week. The same thing happened. Again, I had to meet her again at the coffee shop and then drop her off at the office.

When I got back to the office after the second time meeting, I felt uneasy with this situation. What image was I projecting by meeting up with the same single lady for coffee two weeks in a row and then dropping her off at the office?

I spoke to my wife about it and she shared my concerns. My wife trusted me; she just didn't trust this particular lady. So we agreed that all future meetings would be at the office. If they had to be out of the office, I would send a lady from the office to meet her.

The next time the lady called very excited about our counselling meeting, I insisted on meeting her at the office. I even offered to send one of my staff members to pick her up. I also suggested that I could send one of my lady staff members to pray with her. She said she would call back in a few minutes. Till this day she hasn't called back.

In another incident the church had changed service providers and the manager of the new company we took on offered to take me for lunch at a fancy restaurant, something she said they did with all their new clients in appreciation for the new business. However, the lady pastor in charge of operations, the one who had been the key person in the conversations to change providers and the one who had negotiated the new rates, was not invited. I was surprised and decided to ask the pastor what was going on.

When I told her about the lunch, she told me she had a gut feeling that this lunch was not as innocent as it was made to appear. So we agreed that she would accompany me. As you can imagine, that lunch meeting was awkward, silent and very short. We talked only about business matters.

My point is this: If you don't have boundaries as a leader, you have already set yourself up for failure. "Like a city whose walls are broken through is a person who lacks self-control" (Prov 25:28).

When I was in Bible college, a lecturer named Kilonzo took us through a simple yet wonderful unit on pastoral ministry. It was a very simple two-hour unit that dealt with the very core of what it means to be a shepherd. He mentioned something that has stuck in my heart since then: the three dreaded G's that will bring you down as a pastor – Girls, Gold and Glory.

Girls: Your position gives you access to people's lives, and as a male pastor (I have more experience in this area) who is caring, listening and loving, some ladies will read this the wrong way. They will see and want more than you can give. The really dangerous ones will be like Delilah and will try to entrap you. If you fall into their trap, you will get a very expensive haircut that will cost you your leadership and, even more painful, your relationship with God.

One of the saddest verses I have read over and over again and again to keep myself in check is Judges 16:20:

> Then she called, "Samson, the Philistines are upon you!"
>
> He awoke from his sleep and thought, "I'll go out as before and shake myself free." But he did not know that the LORD had left him.

Samson was confident that he could still fight, and did not recognize that the Lord had already left him.

I am sure the situation must be similar for lady pastors. Some men will look beyond the ministry that is your role and responsibility as a shepherd and see you as a prize to be won or conquered.

If you are married, the first line of defence is a solid marriage and an open honest relationship with your spouse. The Bible says, "Though one may be overpowered, two can defend themselves. A cord of three strands is not quickly broken" (Eccl 4:12).

Our spouses help us see our blind spots. They are able to see danger coming and warn us. As Ecclesiastes says, when you fight as a unit you can defend yourself, but if you try and fight alone, the chances are you will be overpowered.

Male pastors take note: Our wives have an ingrained intuition, a sixth sense that helps them identify predators long before you have realized that you are prey.

It took a long time for me to understand this. At first I thought my wife was just being fussy and insecure, but in almost all the incidents where she was either uncomfortable with someone or suspicious of their intentions, time proved that she was right.

It goes back to first things first; make building your marriage your first ministry priority.

Gold: People will entrust you with their money. They will give towards your vision and mission, and unlike investors in a business they don't expect returns or dividends. As you get access to these monies, you need to remain faithful and full of integrity.

A pastor who has no financial boundaries is on the highway to self-destruction. Money, like anything with great power, can build kingdoms or destroy them. Scripture warns us of this. It's never the amount of money, but the love of money.

> For the love of money is a root of all kinds of evil. Some people, eager for money, have wandered from the faith and pierced themselves with many griefs. (1 Tim 6:10)

I read of pastors caught up in financial scandals and my heart bleeds because this is betrayal of people's faithfulness towards the kingdom.

From the very first time you start dealing with money, you need to intentionally put systems and structures around you that allow for transparency and accountability. This will save your soul.

I know money is a very sensitive topic for pastors, but we need to have this conversation. The love of money will destroy you faster than you can prepare a good sermon. Once you get to a point where there is no clear distinction between your money and church money, you are headed for trouble.

Simple tools like budgets and a finance policy that clearly stipulates how monies are received, used, and accounted for are a good start for accountability. So is having multiple signatories to accounts. I once met a pastor who was the sole signatory to the church account and carried the cheque book with him at all times. That is a disaster waiting to happen.

Glory: Even when you are in a small church somewhere in your "village", there will always be people who hold you in very high regard and believe every word you say. They will shift their lives and make decisions based on what you say.

This is compounded as the church grows. Some pastors start to think that they are the centre of the church or ministry they lead. Soon they are continually looking for that pat on the back. They become the reference point for the ministry or church they lead. The pastor feels as if he is the central force that holds the ministry, church and entire congregation together, and soon he is a small god.

There is a growing trend of what I call "self-ordination", where pastors give themselves titles like "apostle", "bishop" or "prophet" and many more strange ones. I have no personal issues with these titles or with those who want to use them. But I am concerned that these titles have lost the functionality they originally carried and are now used by some as positional titles, based on the size of their church or the size they want to suggest it is to other pastors. Someone plants a church, and when it gets to twenty people they become an apostle! Who are they an apostle to? The twenty? Once you start using titles as a growth strategy, you are missing the point.

Other pastors start to feel that God really needs them so as to accomplish the Great Commission. They feel like God's gift to humanity and their church. Every testimony shared by the congregation is about how the pastor did this and that and about how if it were not for the pastor or his ministry they would have been lost. And so it goes on.

African culture, like many cultures is strong on hero worship; this is reflected in how we treat those above us from our village chief to our politicians and even pastors. And there is definitely a place for showing honour and respect to those above us. The Bible is clear on that: "Give to everyone what you owe them: If you owe taxes, pay taxes; if revenue, then revenue; if respect, then respect; if honour, then honour" (Rom 13:7).

It is when God is pushed to the fringes and we take the centre of the stage that things get out of balance.

When those we lead start to put us on a pedestal, our responsibility is to help them see that we are but stewards and Jesus is the Head of all. Do not be mistaken. You and I can never share God's glory! There is only one God and he is eternal, all-powerful and the earth we live on is merely his footstool. Isaiah declares: "Thus says the LORD: 'Heaven is my throne, and the earth is my footstool; where is the house you will build for me? Where will my resting place be?'" (Isa 66:1).

If you think I am exaggerating, read about what happened to King Nebuchadnezzar who thought he was almost as great as God.

> Twelve months later, as the king was walking on the roof of the royal palace of Babylon, he said, "Is not this the great Babylon I have built as the royal residence, by my mighty power and for the glory of my majesty?"
>
> Even as the words were on his lips, a voice came from heaven, "This is what is decreed for you, King Nebuchadnezzar: Your royal authority has been taken from you. You will be driven away from people and will live with the wild animals; you will eat grass like the ox. Seven times will pass by for you until you acknowledge that the Most High is sovereign over all kingdoms on earth and gives them to anyone he wishes."
>
> Immediately what had been said about Nebuchadnezzar was fulfilled. He was driven away from people and ate grass like the ox. His body was drenched with the dew of heaven

until his hair grew like the feathers of an eagle and his nails like the claws of a bird. (Dan 4:29–33)

It is only after he realized his true place in relation to God that things got back on track:

> At the end of that time, I, Nebuchadnezzar, raised my eyes towards heaven, and my sanity was restored. Then I praised the Most High; I honoured and glorified him who lives forever.
>
> His dominion is an eternal dominion; his kingdom endures from generation to generation. (Dan 4:34)

My wife and I have had this conversation a hundred times or more. Every time we read or watch disturbing news about the fall of wonderful Christian leaders, we take time to reflect and ask ourselves hard questions. Are we living within godly boundaries?

The greatest mistake leaders make is to assume and believe that it would never happen to them; they are okay. That is exactly what the devil wants you to believe.

There are very few people who step into pastoral leadership with the express desire to fall or bring shame to the name of Christ, yet so many do. Why?

Boundaries, boundaries and boundaries. If you live a life without boundaries as a minister, whether it's at home, at work or in the community, you are setting yourself up to fail.

For example, after realizing that a few of the ladies who walk into my office for counselling do so with unhealthy motives, I made sure that the door into my office has a glass panel so anyone in the next office can see me and the person I am talking to. I know that and the person I'm with in the office knows it too.

I have also made it my policy, as much as possible, to counsel a lady only once. Thereafter I either counsel her with my wife present or connect her to a lady in the church to continue the walk. When I have to meet a lady alone in the office and it is someone I do not know well, I have my assistant sit in on the meeting. If it's at a coffee shop, I will ask my assistant to come with me and sit at a table not too far away.

I know some may think this is paranoid or that I have trust issues. But I am not passing a blanket judgment on every lady or gentleman who walks into my office or your office. Not all of them do so with ill intentions. But even if it's only 0.0001% that do, that small insignificant percentage is enough to destroy you, your family and the ministry that God has made you a steward of. So be alert.

Remember Samson in the book of Judges. Delilah gave him a haircut that cost him his physical sight, his ministry as Israel's judge, and ultimately his life.

The greatest mistake you and I can make as pastors (and I am now talking to male pastors) is to think that you are a man of steel and that nothing can move you or bring you down. Always remember that we are all mortals and sin still has a strong pull on us.

God uses the Ten Commandments in Exodus 20:1–17 to set boundaries for the nation of Israel and ultimately for us, because he knows we need them.

So be intentional in building boundaries into your life. Let the Bible always be the guiding factor in how you build them. Other books and articles on boundaries, financial integrity, etc. are great and can offer superb insights and methods, but the word of God should be your ultimate reference point.

10

KEY PLAYERS

Who are the key players in my life and ministry? Who forms the crowd, the centre and the core?

I learnt to ask myself this question long ago, at the time when I was captain of my high school hockey team. There was the first eleven. These were the crucial people who comprised the start team. They had jelled over time and had an inner understanding of how we moved as a unit. We had practised so much together that by instinct we knew what formation to take during a short corner or defensive retreat.

There was one interesting guy on the team named Baluwinder (we just called him Balu). Balu was a big Indian guy who struggled to run a few metres without almost passing out and sweating profusely. To look at him, you would never think that he would be part of the first eleven. But I always chose him.

There were fitter team members, good strikers and excellent defenders. But when you get on the field, what's important is not how well you defended or how skilled your dribbling was, although these do matter. The game and trophy go to the team that scores the most goals. Everything else should work towards that outcome.

Balu had something few of us had; he had an eye for the goal and could strike the ball from any angle with such force and precision it amazed me and put fear in our opponents. All we had to do was ensure the ball got to him while he was in the scoring area. If we did that, we were assured of a goal or an injured goalkeeper. So Balu held the record for the most goals scored by our team in many tournaments.

Going back to the question on key players, every pastor has key players in his or her ministry. These are the people who have bought into the vision "heart and soul". They are your first eleven, so to speak. They are willing to go the extra mile, they understand your heart and are committed for the long haul. They want to see God glorified and the church or ministry grow. These people are very important, especially when a new church is forming or when you are taking up a new leadership role within a church.

Sadly though, as we put together this "first eleven" team – whether they are on staff or lay leaders, deacons, and elders – we often forget the one key player that every pastor needs in his or her corner – his wife or her husband.

As I have said before, a strong marriage and family is your first responsibility and also your first line of defence.

Marriage is hard work. No matter whether you are a fire-breathing prophet or an eloquent charismatic leader of a megachurch, if you are married to a human being, you are bound to go through tough seasons with your spouse. It is our nature, because we are sinners and in our sin and brokenness we get into conflict with one another.

My wife and I attended a marriage seminar early in our marriage that was led by Pastors Muriithi and Carol Wanjau of Mavuno Church. Of all the great things we learnt, one stood out: how to go through the seasons of marriage.

They taught us that marriages go through various seasons each with its blessings and challenges. They focused on four different stages: Dream, Drama, Discovery, and Depth.

I will focus on the first two: Dream and Drama.

The Dream stage is the honeymoon stage that happens very early in marriage. As Pastor Muriithi says, nobody ever marries a real person. They marry a dream, one that they have had since childhood, of a beautiful woman or a handsome man, the Mr Right or Miss Right.

The girls dream of Prince Charming riding on a white horse, dressed in shining armour with a sword at his side. The guys dream of finding a beautiful princess, sweeping her off her feet and riding away with her to live happily ever after.

The Dream stage is when romance and intense attraction bond a couple together and lead to commitment. Passion at this stage is very strong and significant. The Song of Solomon describes this type of relationship when it says, "Strengthen me with raisins, refresh me with apples, for I am faint with love" (Song 2:5).

The chemistry is evident and the couple are emotionally connected. They're fascinated by each other. Without even trying hard, they do things for each other that they would never naturally do by themselves! They also strive to fit into the picture of what society thinks a married couple should look like. If you are a pastor, the pressure to look good is even greater.

I married when I was a youth pastor, and the young people I was pastoring kept on telling us how they prayed that marriage would be like ours. They saw it as beautiful, filled with unending love. That was true, but what they didn't know was that such a marriage takes work, hard work.

Every marriage has a season of darkness and conflict. This stage of Drama begins when you see the light and realize that you and your spouse differ about some things. You find out that you are married to a real person, not a dream or an angel. You both have jobs to attend to, bills to pay, deadlines to meet, in-laws and all the joys and stresses of life to deal with. Not all your conflicts can be easily resolved.

You may find yourself feeling disappointed and thinking you made a wrong choice. You start to feel walls coming up in your marriage and may succumb to a sense of loss, discouragement and even despair. You may even find yourself resenting and blaming your partner and feeling stifled by them. You feel betrayed that they no longer do the things they used to do so effortlessly. Pastor Muriithi shared with us that the biggest complaint from married couples in this season is "he/she no longer does the things he/she used to do!"

I say it once again, as a pastor you are not immune to the challenges of marriage. Leading a church, whatever its size, while navigating in the storms of a challenging marriage is no easy task. The challenges and weight of leading people can consume us and blind us to what really matters – the relationship with our spouse who should always be our key player.

I have met spouses who are bitter at God, the church and everything related to Christ simply because they have been pushed out of the way and neglected. I have met wives who struggle to attend the churches their husbands lead because of the incessant conflict at home. They can't reconcile the man in the pulpit with the man at home.

A pastor's spouse is expected to behave a certain way, remain positive at all times, support their partner in growing the church. Few stop to ask how the spouse is really doing. Everyone just assumes that he or she has bought into the great vision, no questions asked.

One lady told me that she felt like an accessory in her husband's church. She would just sit next to him during service, look happy, say amen, stand next to him after service and smile at people as they left church. But when they got home, things would take a terrible turn because he was a violent and abusive man. Yet every Sunday came she needed to act the part of a good submissive wife. Her husband demanded this.

I have met many pastors' wives, and I have learnt both from them and from my wife that being the pastor's wife can at times be a very lonely place.

Scripture teaches us that God is a covenant-keeping God: "Know therefore that the LORD your God is God; he is the faithful God, keeping his covenant of love to a thousand generations of those who love him and keep his commandments" (Deut 7:9).

God expects the same from us.

Marriage is a covenant and, as in all covenants, both parties have roles and responsibilities. "So they are no longer two, but one flesh. Therefore what God has joined together, let no one separate" (Matt 19:6). There are many things that can break a marriage. But the church cannot and should never be the reason why you broke your marriage covenant.

You have to work hard on your marriage; your wife is your first key player! She is more important than your church-planting team, your deacons or the elders' board, or the women's ministry leader. She is the only person with whom you have a covenant, and a covenant that is only ended by death. All of the others can move to a different church, but you are united to your spouse for life.

Therefore you need to have your spouse at the centre of what you are doing. You need to sound them out about your vision. Your spouse knows you, and can ask the right questions and keep you in check.

I have learnt that my wife (like many pastors' wives) has considerable insight into what is happening in the church. Most of the time, we as pastors are busy dealing with big visions and big budgets. We forget to look down and see what is happening at ground level. Your spouse can help you do this.

If there is one key person you need in your corner, it's your spouse.

You can risk losing a position as a lead pastor or church planter, but never risk losing your marriage; that price is just too high to pay.

So I have learnt that before I get buy-in from the key people in church, before I share my grand church-planting plan with the congregation, I get buy-in from my wife. I want her to be part of the vision. I want her in it not because I am the pastor and she is the pastor's wife but because she believes in it heart and soul.

I have learnt to share my dreams, fears and reflections with my wife. I ask her to pray with and for me. I let her know when we are on a victorious path and when we are in a tough season.

The same is true of your children. Young as they are, they need to be part of the vision. They need to understand what you are willing to live and die for. You will not find a great minister with a broken home or a broken home with a great minister.

As you build your team and identify your key players, make sure that your family, and especially your spouse, is at the top of the list!

11

SWISS KNIFE PASTOR

I was once given a Swiss knife as a gift. I struggled to open it all up to inspect all the little tools tucked away inside. It had a little saw, a small screwdriver, a number of knives and even a magnifying glass. With this gadget you could potentially do a lot of little things but nothing major. The Swiss knife is designed to fit in your pocket and to help get a few things done quickly and conveniently.

That knife made me think. I had reached a point of frustration in my leadership journey. Something was just not working. I needed to know exactly who I was and what I was gifted at. Being in a small team had pushed me to do many little things. I began to think of myself as a Swiss knife pastor – doing a bit of everything until I didn't know exactly what I could do well.

As the church started to grow numerically, I knew that being a Swiss knife pastor was not going to be practical any more. I knew I had to change, and change is always uncomfortable. I didn't know how to go about it. There was a tension between my doing what needed to get done and my passion to do what I was good at.

It was while I was in this state of confusion that I was introduced to Mr Chege. He walked into my office at 7:30 a.m. on a Tuesday morning. This was a meeting I had been looking forward to and dreading. Mr Chege came on the recommendation of one of my pastors.

As he sat down I anxiously wondered whether I had made the right decision. Was I was ready for the truth that this journey would reveal about who I was?

Mr Chege worked for a personal development company that specialized in coaching leaders and pastors. Their aim was to help leaders understand the core of who they are and their gifts. Sometimes this involved stripping away a leader's perceived image of himself or herself and changing their idea of what they do well.

You can see why I was worried. I had made myself vulnerable by agreeing to talk to Mr Chege. What if I have been on the wrong leadership path to begin with? Would I have the energy to press reset and restart?

The process was quite simple. Mr Chege and I would meet twice a month for three months during which he would take me through a rigorous process. This process would involve assessments and talking to my fellow pastors, staff members and those in top leadership within our church. He would also talk with our elders and those outside the church whom I had worked with at some point in the last few years. Even more worrying was the fact that he would also get feedback from some congregation members.

All these individuals would give feedback on my leadership style by filling in an assessment form and sending it directly to Mr Chege. I would therefore not know who said what. I would only get the hard truth about what people truly thought of me as a leader.

Because of the nature of what we do as pastors, very few of us ever hear the hard truth about what type of leader we are. People often struggle to challenge spiritual leaders. They just keep quiet or change churches rather than confront their pastor.

This can have a negative effect in many ways. Misplaced leaders may keep "messing" up as they try to figure out their leadership gifts. In the process people are hurt, teams crumble, churches stagnate, ministries suffer and the Great Commission moves slowly.

As a leader you really need to know your core area of gifting. Knowing this will give you clarity, and clarity allows you to lead more effectively.

In those three months with Mr Chege I learnt three great truths about personal leadership. There is what you think about your leadership capabilities. There is what other people think about your leadership capabilities. And then there is the truth about what you are actually capable of. Knowing how to differentiate between the three while building on each simultaneously is critical for growth.

As a pastor or leader, what people tell you they think about your leadership is not always a true reflection of what they actually believe.

Few people want to put their spiritual leader on the spot by asking hard leadership questions. Many pastors have poured their lives serving those they lead, and people are reluctant to "break" their pastor's heart by telling him that he is not leading well.

Sometimes circumstances force us to take up roles and responsibilities we are not good at, things we can only do to an average level. Then there are things you are naturally good at; you are passionate, energized when you do them. They come naturally to you.

When I began leading and building a youth ministry, I was everything. I had a very small volunteer team that was tied up in the busy life of university. They were always either studying for exams, carrying out class projects, participating in sports, and so on. I couldn't expect much from them except on Sunday mornings. But when they were available, they did great things and carried a lot of weight. For the rest of the time, I was the youth pastor, service leader, outreach coordinator, sound and set-up guy, and at times the music leader.

When I transitioned into leading a small church, the staff team was also small and so I was once again the lead pastor, service planner, accounts expert, procurement officer, small group coordinator, preacher, visitation pastor, and sometimes the set-up guy and much more. This type of situation is common in a small church, where you just can't afford to hire more people. Your congregation is already overstretched so they can't take on more responsibilities. You are forced to take on various roles to keep the church moving. This is the Swiss knife role. At this point in time when the team is small the focus is not so much on getting things done as it is on making it to next Sunday and praying that people come.

Some pastors fit into the Swiss knife role very well. And with time they become good at it. They earn a degree in "jack of all trades" with a minor in "master of none".

However as a ministry grows and people who are actually qualified to do those things start to move into various roles, some pastors struggle to let go. The processes are so entrenched in them or they are the process itself. They want to use a Swiss knife to build a house.

I have learnt a key lesson: You need to know what only you can do that no one else can. If you don't learn this, you will end up frustrating the whole team by meddling in other people's areas of responsibility.

When the team is small and you are the constant point of reference on almost all matters, you start to feel capable of running the entire show. You have your hand in virtually everything. But if you keep doing this as the system gets more complex, you will end up cross-connecting the wires and short-circuiting the system.

I have also learnt that there is a point when you are doing a little bit of everything that you get used to it and start to confuse it with competency. But the fact that you can do all these things does not mean you are good at them. You soon discover this when the team grows and you bring people on board who are actually competent in those fields.

When the church was small, I used to lead the finance meeting every Tuesday morning. We would look at budgets, bank balances, requisitions and expenditure, etc. I have no accounting background save for an Introduction to Accounting course I did in college. But I started to get used to leading these meetings and making decisions. Somehow we managed to muddle through, but our accounts books were nowhere near professional standards.

When Pastor David joined the team, I asked him to help me lead this meeting. I then realized how incompetent I was in this field! He was able to run a meeting that made sense. He could produce reports and help the team differentiate between actual expenses and items on the budget. Pastor David has a degree in economics.

Our account books started to look clean and make more sense. We were now able to track expenditure almost to the cent. This was a great help when we approached banks for financing.

After a few months I left him to lead that team and run that meeting. He also leads our church finance committee. I get a monthly financial report and meet with him bi-weekly so he can bring me up to speed. This is just one example of what happens when you are able to transition from Swiss knife mode.

Mr Chege also helped me negotiate the problem of confusing my ability to get some things done with competence and gifting. The more we went on with the coaching process, the more I realized I actually did not know my core gifts. I had some rough idea of them, but if asked "What are your core gifts?" I could not give a crystal clear answer.

Unfortunately, some of the leadership books I had read had given me a skewed view on leadership. Those books were written by pastors and leaders way ahead of me in the leadership journey. I hadn't matured enough in my leadership to be able to read what they had written and distil what I needed for where I was.

The process was slow and painful. As we met, Mr Chege removed layer after layer of presumptions, assumptions and perceptions. He slowly started to help me see things more clearly. I started to understand the things I was gifted at but not passionate about and the things I was gifted in and passionate about and could grow in.

This process did not increase the giving in our church. Nor could I suddenly hire more staff. What it did was help me focus on my core gifts and lead from a point of strength and clarity. So even as I did the other Swiss knife things that needed to be done, I tried never to lose focus on my core gifts.

I was also able to know whom to have around me. I realized that I am a big picture type of guy, a dreamer, but I really struggle with details. So as I built the team, I knew I had to get people within my circle who love details and logistics or the vision would stall. These individuals would help me see my blind spots and as a team we could get things done faster and more efficiently for the glory of God.

You may be in a church that has just started. If so, you will have to be a jack of all trades for a season. But knowing your gift allows you to focus and know whom to bring around you.

I know not everyone can get access to a development coach or assessment tests and so on. The big lesson here is that you need to know your core gifting. It will bring clarity. The natural thing to do when a church is growing is to get into "get things done" mode. But you have to create time to reflect and remind yourself of what you are gifted and passionate about. Learn to keep these things on your radar even as you do all the other things.

There is a season for being a Swiss knife pastor or leader. If you do not take this role, your ministry or church will suffer. But you cannot be a Swiss knife pastor all your life if you want to be an effective leader. You need to intentionally gather people around you who can speak truthfully into your life. They will help you get clarity as you grow in your role.

12

BUILDING FROM THE GROUND UP

Reading John 1, where we see Jesus recruiting his first disciples, got me thinking about staffing in the church setting.

Jesus is God. He is all-powerful and I am sure he can get things done without human help, so why recruit the twelve? Why spend time going around asking these guys to follow him?

What was he trying to teach us? Because for sure we know he wasn't saying "I need help".

I believe he was teaching a simple yet profound truth, namely that the vision and mission he was setting before us is too big for any one person, church or denomination; it is a God-sized mission. "Go make disciples of *all nations*" – not converts or followers but *disciples*.

No matter how gifted you are, the Great Commission is just too big for any one person. Yes your vision and call must align with it, but to be effective you must have an effective team to work with.

One of my turning points came when it dawned on me that I had to rebuild my staff team based on where I felt the Lord was leading us as a congregation. The only challenge I had was that I did not have the resources to hire the high calibre, top-notch team members who come with superpowers.

I went to one of my mentors and shared my woes about not having money yet needing to build a team. I had interacted with or read books by wonderful pastors doing great things for God and one common factor was they all had great teams. So I really needed one immediately. I had read in leadership and business books that without a great team you would struggle. I was struggling. My unfortunate reality was that we were struggling to meet budget every month.

Well, that was my biggest problem. I wanted a team immediately, here and now. If I could have got a team in a packet and microwaved them I would have done it. I would have liked to walk into a supermarket and ask on which row they kept the freshly stocked super-teams.

After trying to unsuccessfully convince my mentors that the issue was my lack of money, they patiently guided me back to the core issue. I wanted a solid, motivated and effective team without building one.

They had been in ministry for years and had built their teams over the years.

Going back to John 1: Jesus being the Son of God had the authority and capability to call into his team the best players of his time – the religious teachers that Israel could offer.

It reminded me of when we played soccer in primary school and we had to choose the teams. The two best players would always be the captains, and they would toss a coin to determine who chose first. The rest of us would line up and they would start calling the best guys one after another. As the line got shorter, the choosing was based more on mercy than skill. Everyone hated to be the last guy who had to join a side because there was no one else left to pick.

I was feeling like the guy who had to choose last because I didn't have the resources to pick the best. So once again I tried to talk to my mentors about my money challenges.

My lack of money pitch to build a great team ended at a breakfast meeting. I was sitting across the table from one of my mentors, again lamenting the lack of funds, when he said, "It is always best to build your team from the ground up."

He shared with me the challenges of hiring what he called "stars". They had caused him much grief because they came with a set way of doing things. Their reputation preceded them and they often had unrealistic expectations. Most of them would do well in a church where systems and processes were already in place and functioning. But in growing congregations with very fluid systems (if any), stars became a stress factor.

At that time, our church was nowhere near having systems and processes. We were at the point of getting Sunday done and hoping a few more people would come.

I decided to read a bit more about recruitment in some of the biggest churches that have had a great impact the world over. To my amazement, I discovered that the core of the top leadership for most of these churches had been together for years, sometimes for decades. They had started together and grown together.

This is where I learnt the principle that when you are starting, you build your team from the ground up. This allows you to set the tone and boundaries and, most importantly, define the culture.

You want a great team – build one, don't buy one. Jesus took the lowliest of men and in three years turned them into great pillars of faith. They grew from unknown fishermen to custodians of the greatest story.

There was something else I learnt as I thought about Jesus and his disciples. The problem that was bothering me was how do you hire people when you don't have money to pay what everyone else pays? So how did Jesus persuade the disciples to follow him for three years and after that be willing to give heart and soul to his cause even if it meant death? The answer is that he called them to a vision not a salary.

Jesus used very simple terms in his job interview: "Come follow me and I will make you fishers of men." There was no promise of great wealth, extended leave, a corner office, top-notch medical cover, or a year-end bonus. No, all he offered was becoming fishers of men. He simply said "I am going to change the world. Do you want to be part of it?"

What Jesus was calling these men into was a great vision, something greater than themselves. He showed them how big it was and that they could be part of it.

I have learnt that when building a team, the benefits of calling people to a vision far outweigh the benefits of a better salary. (Note: I am not suggesting that you don't pay your staff well!)

I was once told, good leaders are hard to find, and when you do find them, keep them! What makes exceptional people stay? Is it a salary increment or a title? I have found that when people are part of something great, and they find their place in that greatness, they will stay. Another employer can always outbid you on the salary, but loyalty, passion and commitment are hard to buy or bid on.

You can only call people to be part of something that you believe in heart and soul. When I joined Nairobi Chapel, one of the key reasons I joined was the vision. When Pastor Oscar shared the 2020 vision, I saw myself in it. My heartbeat accelerated at the thought of being part of something so big for God. Witness to 1,000,000 people, disciple 10,000 converts, and plant 300 churches!

I said to myself this is what I have been looking for, a cause to believe in, something worth fighting for. So when the job offer came, the line with starting salary was not at all attractive (given that I had just married), but it did not in any way dampen my passion to be part of the great vision of global church planting.

I started to reflect on the process of building from the ground up, and where we were going. I knew I had to restructure the team I had inherited before I could start building it up. It was comprised of great people who loved the Lord as much as I did. Some were great friends even outside the office environment. However, we were not all in sync in terms of vision and strategy.

As the vision became clearer and roles were redefined and new roles emerged, it became quite clear that I would need to rebuild the team to align with this new direction. I pondered night and day on how I would go about this difficult task. Then at one of our lead pastor's meetings, Pastor Oscar shared on the 5 C's of hiring. This was the matrix he used when getting new staff members. This was an answer to my prayer and would form the grid I would use in reengineering the team.

The 5 C's are Character, Competence, Chemistry, Capacity and Calling.

I decided to focus on the three most important for the situation I was in: Chemistry, Competence and Capacity. I could ignore Calling and Character because I already knew that the team members had responded to God's call to serve in the kingdom. They were also all men and women of great character.

The first C that was critical to me was thus *Chemistry*. This is something that is hard to define in words. How do you measure chemistry in a team or person?

I decided to ask myself, whom do I feel connected to in the team? With whom do I click so that our conversations go beyond the office? You can tell when you have chemistry with someone.

I have often gone to new places and met a group of strangers. With some of them, I click effortlessly and we end up talking about things that really matter to both of us. With others, I struggle to keep a conversation going; it just doesn't take off. It's not that they are bad people; we just don't click.

I knew that there were some people on my team with whom I could never develop a relationship that would grow beyond a working relationship that was based on tasks and objectives. Such relationships are fine in the corporate and business world, but in the pastoral arena you are more than just co-workers; you are brothers and sisters under the lordship of Christ. Our relationships have to go beyond the tasks and objectives.

The second C in my grid was *Competence*. Once I was clear on where we were heading and the type of growth that would come, I asked myself who, based on past experience and interactions, had the ability to get things done? I knew that there were some in the team who had struggled in the past, and I knew that they would struggle in this new endeavour.

And finally *Capacity*. Who has the emotional, psychological and spiritual capacity to step into a new venture and give their best regardless of the circumstances? For the next two years the church was going to be going through constant change as we worked to cast a new vision and realign to that new vision. From my time in youth ministry, I had learnt that not everyone handles constant change very well. Some people like a systematic and predictable way of doing things, and that was not what we were going to have for the next few years.

After spending time in prayer and reflection, I felt it was time to begin the hard conversations.

This is when you learn that being a lone ranger for Jesus is not a good idea. It is also when you see the blessing of being part of a larger family, which for me was the Nairobi Chapel.

First, I sent word out asking if any of the chapel churches were looking to hire anyone or knew anyone in their extended networks that was looking for good people. I got responses with openings. (I don't know if this was just good timing or the Lord showing mercy. I tend to think the latter.)

Then I had conversations with those I knew could do great things for the kingdom if placed in a different environment. I met with them and shared where we were going and got their feedback. These were very hard and uncomfortable conversations. I made a decision not to rush through them.

As we met more and spoke more and things became clearer, most of the conversation went well. A number of my team members took up positions in other churches.

These types of conversations go differently when you let someone know you believe in them and have taken the time to seek out opportunities within the body of Christ for them to consider. Then such conversations can be affirming, rather than devastating.

I also chose to pay them a few months extra salary to help them settle and adjust to their new jobs.

Some of the conversations went really badly. No matter how hard I tried and no matter what I put on the table, some just didn't see what I saw. They thought they had a right to be on the team, regardless of the changes that were coming. Some had been on the team longer than me and liked things the way they were. Making the decision to let them go was hard. Some of those hard decisions cost me some relationships, but I knew it had to be done.

There is no magic ingredient for building good teams fast. It takes time. If you intend to lead for the long haul, then build your team from the ground up.

13

TEAM OR FAMILY?

As the team forms, one the thing that forms with it is culture. Knowingly or unknowingly, you will build a culture among your staff. So before starting to build a team, you need to answer these questions: What type of team do I want? What values do I want to uphold? What role will I take?

I too had to think carefully about these things. Would my key focus be on it as a team or as a family? Was there too much familiarity? Or were we too distant? At what point do we stop being a family and become a staff team? Can we be both family and team? What role should I take up? Team leader or shepherd? Could I be both?

In a family setting, all the members have one reference point – the parents. All the siblings share a common bond, whether they love each other or not. For a team, it's different. The members all come from different backgrounds and the only point of common reference is the team leader.

As the leader you may have good chemistry with each team member. But that does not mean that there is also good chemistry between the team members. For a team to function well there needs to be clarity about roles, responsibilities and expectations. In the family setting the common point of reference (your parents) hopefully helps you to clarify roles, responsibilities and expectations. The same needs to be true for a team regardless of their different backgrounds.

The challenge is finding balance between being a team and a family. I have seen church staff teams that did not clarify these roles and soon the team was overtaken and overwhelmed by confusion, unrealistic expectations and a lot of hurt.

Some of the teams I have interacted with are purely a workforce. They get things done. The emphasis is on deliverables. You are on the team to fulfil a specific role. And once you are not fulfilling that role, your place in the team is in jeopardy.

These teams are highly effective and definitely get things done. I admire them for this. But the downside is that in most of these teams there is very little emphasis on or concern for relationships. The team is held together by the task that needs to be done.

I have also seen teams that lean heavily towards a family set-up. These teams share a lot of time together, they eat together and there is genuine concern for each other. The work relationships go beyond the office to the team members' homes, children and spouses. These teams value relationship over tasks, and hence there is a great danger of things not getting done. It is hard for the leader to fire someone because the relational implications are far-reaching.

Many young leaders are reading great business books on staffing and implementing HR truths in their teams without processing the impact in their context. I don't know how it works in the business and corporate world, but I guess when you remove the spiritual leadership angle, the lines become a bit clearer.

I continually found myself caught between two confusing roles. I was the pastor not only to the congregation but also to my team. However, I was also the team's "boss" at the office.

A look at Scripture helped me to find a balance between these two roles.

First, Scripture teaches that we are all equal before the Lord and are all under one head, Jesus Christ. So our leadership role does not give us a higher standing before God. Even as custodians or drivers of a vision we have no higher standing before God.

Secondly, Jesus has given us all the same mission objective. Our mandate as pastors, team members, elders and congregation is to fulfil the Great Commission. We exist to share the great story that God loves us so much that he sent his Son Jesus to die in our place and that only in him can we find eternal life.

This truth may be captured in different vision or mission statements for we all operate in different cultures and contexts and have access to different resources. So we may all end up using different strategies to pursue the same goal.

But while our strategies may be different, there are things that need to remain the same. For example we are to be good stewards of the resources God has given us. Money is one such resource.

When people join a staff team and are paid a salary, the stakes are higher. This is because good stewardship requires that when we invest, we get returns. One of the ways we get returns is when paid staff do what they are supposed to do. We have to be workers who are worth our wage.

Jesus teaches this clearly in the Parable of the Talents. He expects us to be good stewards, and good stewards bring returns.

When we do not do what we are supposed to do, or are not doing it well, then good stewardship demands we ask tough questions.

> Then the man who had received one bag of gold came. "Master," he said, "I knew that you are a hard man, harvesting where you have not sown and gathering where you have not scattered seed. So I was afraid and went out and hid your gold in the ground. See, here is what belongs to you."
>
> His master replied, "You wicked, lazy servant! So you knew that I harvest where I have not sown and gather where I have not scattered seed? Well then, you should have put my money on deposit with the bankers, so that when I returned I would have received it back with interest." (Matt 25:24–27)

However, on the other hand, we are pastors and shepherds of those God has placed under our care, including our staff team. We have a responsibility to nurture and care for the teams we lead. At the centre of shepherding and pastoring is love. That is why the Good Shepherd will leave the ninety-nine to look for the one that is lost.

Craig Hamilton in his book *Wisdom in Leadership* says, "To lead a team you need to genuinely love them. If you're going to lead them you need to serve them. If you're going to serve them and want them to succeed, you will need to love them."[1]

---

[1] Craig Hamilton, *Wisdom in Leadership* (Waterloo, NSW: Matthias Media, 2015), 171.

Everything in your leadership is about love. As a pastor love for the Father and the lost is the fuel that drives us in ministry. It should also drive how we lead our teams.

After much pondering, I decided that we would be a team that operated on family values and principles. So the first thing I did was to establish a routine of eating together. From my own experience I knew that some of the deepest and most memorable conversations happen around the dinner table.

The individual team members had either been going out to restaurants for lunch or eating a packed lunch they had brought with them. Now I asked the office to arrange for someone to either deliver lunch or to cook lunch for us at the church. I then told the team that the office would be providing a healthy lunch at a highly subsidized cost. But there was one condition. The food would be served in one location and no one was allowed to eat in their office.

We then began to meet in the basement for lunch. When we started it was quite awkward. People would eat quickly and leave. Many wanted to finish and "get back to work". However, as the people began to relax, conversations started picking up. I would often ask a life question that we would talk through as we ate.

It was in this place that I started to shape and define the culture of our small team through conversations. I would share what I loved and the things that made me turn red, green or blue. I would also learn what other people were passionate about or struggled with.

As the team grew, this style of lunch became a norm for the new staff members. We eat together and talk about life. This is the place I get to know where people are in life. Who has been engaged or has started dating, who has moved house or is saving up to buy a TV. From the most mundane of things to the most complicated things like broken relationships.

Looking back I cherish the many lunches we have had as a family. The team has shared great moments, tears and laughter. We are a family.

A team that cannot function like a family will really struggle. There is great joy and fulfilment when you work with friends.

Jesus did this effortlessly. He was a firm leader to his disciples and yet was still their shepherd. He ate and laughed with them, and yet he rebuked them for their unbelief. He was vulnerable before them as the cross drew near, and yet he showed strength in many miracles like the calming of the storm ...

If you and I are going to build a team that will fearlessly take the Great Commission to every corner of the globe, we need strong teams. If the team is weak on relationships, you will simply multiply tasks. If the team is weak in getting things done, you will simply multiply mediocrity. The unhealthy culture you breed as you multiply and grow will at some point become a hindrance to the Great Commission.

Though the team functions as a family, there is need for accountability. Our Lord requires good stewardship of his resources.

The way that worked for us was to build systems and process around the team. These allowed for everyone to function with clarity about their role. These systems and process also allowed for an objective review of what each of us was supposed to be doing. So each person who joined the team had a clear role definition and an understanding of what needed to be done by when. These objectives were constantly reviewed by a supervisor, with two major reviews in the year.

It is in our practice to allow every team member to creatively seek to reach his or her goals and targets. But everyone knows that they will be called to account.

Sadly there are people we have had to let go from the team, and this hurts the family. But this is part of leadership and growth.

14

THE HARVEST IS PLENTIFUL

There are many things that can make us different as churches. However, there are also many things that bring us together. Regardless of traditions, rituals, music or preaching styles, all groups that gather in the name of Christ have two key things in common. If they lack these two things, then I am not sure how to classify them.

The first thing we all have in common is a belief in the Great Commission. We all know that we are called to share the message of the cross and make disciples of those who believe. We are to boldly tell the world that there are eternal consequences if one chooses to reject God. Secondly, we all know that we are to live out the Great Commandment by striving to live in harmony in the community where God has placed us. This does not mean that we live a life of compromise, but rather one that reflects Christ in every sense. As believers these two aspects of the faith should drive how we live every day.

The early believers in the Book of Acts are an example of what happens when individuals, churches and communities live out this truth. There is growth and transformation, the things every pastor prays for and seeks.

We look at transformation of the disciples, who went from being fishermen and tax collectors to individuals entrusted with doctrine and the birth of the church. The early church also grew numerically in ways that defy modern church growth. "Those who accepted his message were baptized, and about three thousand were added to their number that day" (Acts 2:41).

This was the common testimony in the early church. "So the churches were strengthened in the faith and grew daily in numbers" (Acts 16:5). This is the type of report every pastor around the world wants to give at an annual general meeting. A church that loves the community shares Jesus continually and grows exponentially.

If we are going to experience this type of growth, we must have a mind shift in how we view our world. We need to see the world and those who are seeking as Jesus saw them:

> Jesus went through all the towns and villages, teaching in their synagogues, proclaiming the good news of the kingdom and healing every disease and sickness. When he saw the crowds, he had compassion on them, because they were harassed and helpless, like sheep without a shepherd. Then he said to his disciples, "The harvest is plentiful but the workers are few. Ask the Lord of the harvest, therefore, to send out workers into his harvest field." (Matt 9:35–38)

When we take this perspective, we as pastors can stop competing for members. Congregants' moving from one church to another is not church growth. As pastors we sometimes jealously guard those in our congregation. It is important to hold people close as you shepherd them, but don't hold them too tightly. There will always be a church that is doing one thing or other better than you are. And your congregation members will want to go there. When someone has heard about Jesus and made a decision to follow Christ, we have a responsibility to disciple them. But should they choose to leave, don't be over-zealous in trying to stop them. It's hard to lead people who don't want to be where you are. Rejoice that their name is written in the book of life and move on.

Many find it very hard to see the harvest as Jesus saw it. How did Jesus see it? Jesus saw how vast the harvest field was. "Then he [Jesus] said to his disciples, 'The harvest is plentiful'" (Matt 9:37).

The world is big and there are many people. I love looking at the Worldometers website, which shows you the current world population and updates it in real time. When I last looked, the world population was 7.3 billion. That gives me perspective of the vastness of the harvest field! It shakes me loose when I become consumed with the small world I inhabit. When Jesus says the harvest is plentiful, he means plentiful – it is and will always be plentiful.

Think about the country, town or village you live in. The number of people there who are in great need of Christ is overwhelming. Ask yourself how big your church is and what percentage of the lost you are reaching?

Once you ask that question, fighting over congregants should be the last item on your agenda. If as leaders we can focus primarily on those outside the kingdom, a lot will change. We will see how vast the opportunities are and how little we have done.

Jesus sees not only the harvest of people as vast, but also as something that brings tears to his eyes. "When he saw the crowds, he had compassion on them" (Matt 9:36). All those people, then and now, matter to him.

Jesus loves people – this is the central message of why he came, and this is what the cross symbolizes.

It saddens my heart when I read, watch or interact with pastors who have no love for the lost or have forgotten the love they had when they first started serving and leading. They care only about themselves. You can tell they don't love the lost because of the things they do. Ezekiel prophesied about such people:

> The word of the LORD came to me: "Son of man, prophesy against the shepherds of Israel; prophesy and say to them: 'This is what the Sovereign LORD says: Woe to you shepherds of Israel who only take care of yourselves! Should not shepherds take care of the flock? You eat the curds, clothe yourselves with the wool and slaughter the choice animals, but you do not take care of the flock. You have not strengthened the weak or healed the sick or bound up the injured. You have not brought back the strays or searched for the lost. You have ruled them harshly and brutally. So they were scattered because there was no shepherd, and when they were scattered they became food for all the wild animals. My sheep wandered over all the mountains and on every high hill. They were scattered over the whole earth, and no one searched or looked for them.'"
> (Ezek 34:1–6)

This is a true description of what is happening in many churches around the globe. Self-appointed prophets, bishops, and men and women of God have intentionally decided to take advantage of those under their care. They rob their followers in the name of God, they promise on behalf of God, they have appointed themselves mediators between people and God. They are charlatans, seeking only to enrich themselves and build their little kingdoms.

The Apostle Peter in his second letter warns us against such people, saying

> These people are springs without water and mists driven by a storm. Blackest darkness is reserved for them. For they mouth empty, boastful words and, by appealing to the lustful desires of the flesh, they entice people who are just escaping from those who live in error. They promise them freedom, while they themselves are slaves of depravity – for "people are slaves to whatever has mastered them". (2 Pet 2:17–19)

Unfortunately, we who follow them and heed their passionate calls have abandoned our spiritual responsibilities. We have stopped reading the word of God for ourselves and trust others to do it for us and tell us what God is saying. We have stopped listening to the Holy Spirit and are listening to the voices of those around us. In our immature and desperate search for miracles and quick fixes, we pursue miracles by abandoning the God of all miracles. We started to see trials and suffering as strange to the life of a disciple and look for any means to escape any form of trial or suffering.

Jesus described the crowd as being "harassed and helpless, like sheep without a shepherd" (Matt 9:36). This is very true today. People are living in desperation and life seems to be getting more complicated with each passing day. That is one of the reasons people follow false teachers who promise an immediate end to suffering. People are willing to give their earthly possessions to individuals who promise them true happiness. They are walking down a path that leads to death. Jesus says

> Enter through the narrow gate. For wide is the gate and broad is the road that leads to destruction, and many enter through it. But small is the gate and narrow the road that leads to life, and only a few find it. (Matt 7:13–14)

As pastors and leaders we are called to stand firm against the growing threat of false teachers. A time will come when they will be judged. The Bible is very clear about what will happen.

We, on the other hand, need to be a very different kind of leader, the kind who portray the quality that is central to our Lord Jesus – love. Love is the key to good leadership. When you love God as a leader, you will shun evil. When you love God as a leader, you will love those that God loves, seek those that are lost and defend the truth. Love compels us to be faithful to those we lead, faithful to those we serve with and faithful to the message.

We have a responsibility to tell people that they can find true rest in Jesus. This is a great and noble call. We need to remember the words of the Apostle Paul, who was a pastor of pastors:

> For Christ's love compels us, because we are convinced that one died for all, and therefore all died. And he died for all, that those who live should no longer live for themselves but for him who died for them and was raised again. So from now on we regard no one from a worldly point of view. Though we once regarded Christ in this way, we do so no longer. Therefore, if anyone is in Christ, the new creation has come: The old has gone, the new is here! All this is from God, who reconciled us to himself through Christ and gave us the ministry of reconciliation: that God was reconciling the world to himself in Christ, not counting people's sins against them. And he has committed to us the message of reconciliation. We are therefore Christ's ambassadors, as though God were making his appeal through us. We implore you on Christ's behalf: Be reconciled to God. God made him who had no sin to be sin for us, so that in him we might become the righteousness of God. (2 Cor 5:14–21)

Those words have been an anchor in my leadership journey. They help me remember that love should always compel me. That in all I do my core message should always be that one died for all and in him is life eternal. And that I no longer live for myself but for the one who died for me.

We have been entrusted with a noble task of ambassadorship for the Most High God. Let us remain faithful!